Leith's Book of Baking

Leith's Book of Baking

BY
PRUE LEITH
&
CAROLINE WALDEGRAVE

First published in Great Britain 1993
Bloomsbury Publishing Limited, 2 Soho Square,
London W1V 5DE

Copyright © 1993 by Prue Leith and Caroline Waldegrave

The moral right of the authors has been asserted

A CIP catalogue record for this book
is available from the British Library

ISBN 0 7475 1316 3

10 9 8 7 6 5 4 3 2 1

Edited and designed by
Toucan Books Limited, London

Photographer: Andrea Heselton
Assisted by: Sarah Mac, Nesa Mladjenovic
Stylists: Roisin Nield, Sue Russell
Home economists: Polly Tyrer,
Fiona Trail Stevenson, Jackie Brewer,
Puff Fairclough, Janey Bevan
Assisted by: Louise Bacon

Line drawings by Kate Simunek

Printed in Great Britain by The Bath Press, Avon

Contents

Introduction

When we were asked to make a collection of recipes for a baking book we had to decide what we meant by baking. We initially thought to include savoury flans and pies but eventually decided that baking meant breads, buns, pastries, biscuits and scones. However, we have included a couple of our favourite savoury dishes and they are included at the end of the book.

At Leith's School we teach a lot of different techniques but bread-making and cake-making are at the heart of most of the courses we run. If you can make a good génoise cake you have acquired all the necessary manipulative skills to become an excellent cook. Good bread-making is not only an essential in itself, but when you fill the house with the glorious smell of well-made bread you are also showing that you have passed one of the tests of becoming a real cook.

Prue and I feel particularly indebted to Fiona Burrell at Leith's School. She knows so much about baking and has been an enormous help in the production of this book.

I do hope that you will enjoy cooking the recipes. The recipes for this book have all been taken from *Leith's Cookery Bible*.

Caroline Waldegrave

Acknowledgements

This book is officially by Prue Leith and me. In fact this is not really true. Teachers, students and friends of Leith's School of Food and Wine alike have all contributed. Recipes have been unashamedly adapted from magazines, newspaper articles and other cookery books. If we can remember the original source for a recipe we have credited the person involved, but sometimes I'm afraid we no longer know where they came from and hope that their creators will forgive us.

I would particularly like to acknowledge the work of the following people: Fiona Burrell, Alison Cavaliero, Richard Harvey, Charlotte Lyon, Sally Procter, Sarah Staughton, Barbara Stevenson, Lesley Waters and Caroline Yates.

I would also like to thank all those involved in the production of this book, particularly Robert Sackville West at Toucan Books who calmly and charmingly worked so hard on our behalf.

Caroline Waldegrave

All about Cooking

CONVERSION TABLES
The tables below are approximate, and do not conform in all respects to the official conversions, but we have found them convenient for cooking.

Weight

Imperial	Metric	Imperial	Metric
$1/4$oz	7-8g	$1/2$oz	15g
$3/4$oz	20g	1oz	30g
2oz	55g	3oz	85g
4oz ($1/4$lb)	110g	5oz	140g
6oz	170g	7oz	200g
8oz ($1/2$lb)	225g	9oz	255g
10oz	285g	11oz	310g
12oz ($3/4$lb)	340g	13oz	370g
14oz	400g	15oz	425g
16oz (1lb)	450g	$1^1/4$lb	560g
$1^1/2$ lb	675g	2lb	900g
3lb	1.35 kg	4lb	1.8 kg
5lb	2.3 kg	6lb	2.7 kg
7lb	3.2 kg	8lb	3.6 kg
9lb	4.0 kg	10lb	4.5 kg

Liquid measures

Imperial	ml	fl oz
$1^3/4$ pints	1000 (1 litre)	35
1 pint	570	20
$3/4$ pint	425	15
$1/2$ pint	290	10
$1/3$ pint	190	6.6
$1/4$ pint (1 gill)	150	5
	56	2
2 scant tablespoons	28	1
1 teaspoon	5	

Lengths

Imperial	Metric
$1/2$in	1cm
1in	2.5cm
2in	5cm
6in	15cm
12in	30cm

Oven temperatures

°C	°F	Gas mark
70	150	$1/4$
80	175	$1/4$
100	200	$1/2$
110	225	$1/2$
130	250	1
140	275	1
150	300	2
170	325	3
180	350	4
190	375	5
200	400	6
220	425	7
230	450	8
240	475	8
250	500	9
270	525	9
290	550	9

Approximate American/European conversions

Commodity	USA	Metric	Imperial
Flour	1 cup	140g	5oz
Caster and granulated sugar	1 cup	225g	8oz
Caster and granulated sugar	2 level tablespoons	30g	1oz
Brown sugar	1 cup	170g	6oz
Butter/margarine/lard	1 cup	225g	8oz
Sultanas/raisins	1 cup	200g	7oz
Currants	1 cup	140g	5oz
Ground almonds	1 cup	110g	4oz
Golden syrup	1 cup	340g	12oz
Uncooked rice	1 cup	200g	7oz

NOTE: In American recipes, when quantities are stated as spoons, 'level' spoons are meant. English recipes (and those in this book) call for rounded spoons except where stated otherwise. This means that 2 American tablespoons equal 1 English tablespoon.

Useful measurements

Measurement	Metric	Imperial
1 American cup	225ml	8 fl oz
1 egg	56ml	2 fl oz
1 egg white	28ml	1 fl oz
1 rounded tablespoon flour	30g	1oz
1 rounded tablespoon cornflour	30g	1oz
1 rounded tablespoon sugar	30g	1oz
2 rounded tablespoons breadcrumbs	30g	1oz
2 level teaspoons gelatine	8g	$1/4$ oz

30g/1oz granular (packet) aspic sets 570ml (1 pint) liquid.

15g/$1/2$oz powdered gelatine, or 4 leaves, will set 570ml (1 pint) liquid.

(However, in hot weather, or if the liquid is very acid, like lemon juice, or if the jelly contains solid pieces of fruit and is to be turned out of the dish or mould, 20g/$3/4$oz should be used.)

Wine quantities

Imperial	ml	fl oz
Average wine bottle	730	25
1 glass wine	100	3
1 glass port or sherry	70	2
1 glass liqueur	45	1

Bread-Making

Bread-Making

With the advent of factory-made bread, bread-making became, for a while, almost a lost art amongst home cooks. Recently it has become a rediscovered craft and many people make the time to produce their own bread. Bread-making can be improved by understanding what is happening to the dough as it rises and cooks and what factors affect it. Once the process is understood, the cook can branch out from plain white bread to breads that contain nuts, herbs, fruits, vegetables, cheeses and different seeds and grains.

YEAST

Baker's yeast, the most usual leavening agent for bread, is a single-celled organism that belongs to the fungus family. For yeast to reproduce it needs warmth, moisture and food. Given the right conditions it can reproduce very quickly, giving off carbon dioxide as it does so. This is trapped in the dough or batter and so aerates it. The optimum temperature for yeast to reproduce is 25°C/80°F. Too much heat can kill it so care must be taken to ensure that the liquid used in making bread is lukewarm. A high concentration of sugar, fat or salt can slow down its rate of reproduction. If a dough is high in these ingredients then more yeast must be used. There are three types of yeast available: fresh, dried and easy-blend dried yeast.

Fresh yeast should be beige, crumbly-soft and sweet-smelling. It is usually thought of as the most satisfactory form of baker's yeast as it is less likely to produce 'beery' bread. Fresh yeast keeps for five days or so wrapped loosely in the refrigerator, and can be frozen for short periods, though results after freezing are unpredictable. If it is difficult to obtain, use dried yeast, or buy fresh yeast in a suitable quantity, divide it into 30g/1oz pieces, wrap them individually, then overwrap and freeze. Use as soon as the yeast thaws, and do not keep frozen for more than a month.

Dried yeast is bought in granular form in airtight sachets. It will remain active for about six months in a cool dry place. If substituting dried for fresh yeast when following a recipe, halve the weight of yeast called for. Dried yeast takes slightly longer to work than fresh yeast, and must first be 'sponged' in liquid, partly to reconstitute it, partly to check that is is still active. To avoid any beery taste, use rather less than the amount of dried yeast called for and allow a long rising and proving time. Using too much yeast generally means too fast a rise, resulting in bread with a coarse texture that goes stale quickly.

Easy-blend dried yeast is mixed directly with the flour, not reconstituted in liquid first. Sold in small airtight packages, it is usually included in bought bread mixtures. One 7g/¹/₄oz package usually equals 15g/¹/₂oz conventional dried yeast or 30g/1oz fresh yeast.

FLOUR

Flour is the main ingredient in bread and gives it its individual character. Wheat flour is the most common because it contains a large amount of gluten, a form of protein that absorbs liquid to produce elastic strands in the dough. As the yeast works, it gives off carbon dioxide, which is trapped in the expanding dough, making it rise and puff up. When the loaf is cooked and set rigidly, the gas leaks out and is replaced by air.

RYE, MAIZE, MILLET and other flours contain less gluten than wheat flour. Because these flours lack the essential elasticity of wheat gluten, some wheat flour is usually added to the dough to produce a light-textured, well-risen loaf.

WHITE FLOUR is ground from wheat with the outer bran and inner germ removed, leaving 70-75 per cent of the original wheat. Removing the wheatgerm means the flour keeps longer, while removing the bran makes the flour lighter and finer. On the other hand, it will have fewer vitamins. For this reason white flours, whether bleached or unbleached, have B vitamins and other nutrients added to them in most countries. With or without such additions, bread made from white flour will have less flavour and less fibre than that made from wholegrain flour.

STRONG FLOUR is white flour made from varieties of wheat known as 'hard' wheat, which contain a particularly high proportion of gluten. Also called bread flour, the best comes from North America and is usually known as durum wheat. It is highly suitable for bread-making, giving the dough a remarkable capacity to expand and rise and produce a light, well-risen, springy loaf.

WEAK, SOFT OR HOUSEHOLD FLOUR is made from wheat grown mainly in Europe. It has less expansive gluten, produces a less elastic dough and bakes to a heavier, more crumbly bread. It makes excellent cakes and biscuits, where crumbliness and non-elasticity are advantages.

PLAIN FLOUR is general, all-purpose flour claimed to be suitable for sauces, cakes and breads, even though it does not have the high gluten content of strong flour. In Europe, where plain flour contains more soft wheat, it is less suitable for making breads than the plain or all-purpose flour used in North America, which contains more hard wheat.

SELF-RAISING FLOUR is usually made from soft wheat. A raising agent – usually a mixture of bicarbonate of soda and cream of tartar – is mixed with the flour. It is not used in yeast cookery, though some 'breads', such as wholemeal soda bread, are made with it.

WHOLEMEAL OR WHOLEWHEAT FLOUR is milled from the whole grain so that it contains the germ and the bran. Most of the B vitamins are in the wheatgerm, while bran provides roughage necessary for the digestive system. Bread made from wholemeal flour is undoubtedly healthier, but regardless of its natural gluten, it produces a heavier loaf. Also, the oil in the wheatgerm means that wholemeal bread will not keep as well as a white loaf. A mixture of wholemeal and white flour is a good compromise.

STONEGROUND FLOUR is usually wholemeal flour that has been milled between stone rollers rather than by modern milling methods. It is a coarser and heavier flour, even in its white version, than factory-milled flour, so more yeast or a longer rising time is needed to make it rise. It is claimed that more of the wheat's nutrients are retained as the grain is kept cooler during stone-grinding.

WHEATMEAL FLOUR should, judging by its name, refer to any wheat flour. However, the term is used by commercial bakers to describe brown bread flour that is not wholemeal. The colour may simply come from dye. Containing little or no bran or wheatgerm, it makes a lighter loaf. It is usually no more nutritious or 'healthy' than refined white flour.

OTHER BREAD INGREDIENTS

LIQUIDS. For plain everyday bread the only liquid needed is water. It gives a crisp crust and a fairly hard or chewy bread. Milk produces a softer bread and a golden crust and is said by some to increase the keeping quality of bread. Beer gives the bread an individual, malty taste.

SALT is very important in bread. Not only does it affect the flavour but also the rising action of the yeast, the texture of the loaf and the crust. Without salt the flavour of the loaf can be bland. If a quick rising time is required, more yeast and less salt are needed, as in a pizza dough for example. If a dough does not seem to be rising very fast it is worth tasting it. If it tastes noticeably salty, the dough will produce a tough, badly risen loaf.

SUGAR is often included in savoury recipes for bread as a starter for the yeast. Too much sugar retards the yeast however, so sweet doughs usually have a high proportion of yeast. White, demerara and brown sugars are used in doughs as well as molasses, black treacle and golden syrup. Honey can be substituted for golden syrup.

FATS added to a yeast dough include butter, lard, oil and vegetable fats. Butter gives a very good flavour and a good-looking crust. It can impede the action of the yeast and so a dough that is heavily enriched with butter, e.g. brioche dough, may not rise as much as an ordinary dough. Oil makes bread wonderfully easy to knead even when added in small quantities, for example 30ml/2 tablespoons to 675g/1^{1}/2lb flour. Olive oil is the best oil to use, but alternatives are sunflower, peanut or sesame oils.

STAGES IN BREAD-MAKING

It is important to create the right conditions for the yeast to grow so that the dough will be elastic and accommodate the maximum carbon dioxide.

1. If the yeast is fresh, first cream it in a warm, not hot, cup with about 5ml/1 teaspoonful of sugar until smooth, then with a spoonful of lukewarm water. Dried yeast should be mixed with a little sweetened lukewarm water and left in a warm place for about 15 minutes. Once the yeast liquid is frothy, or 'sponges', add it to the flour, and mix in any remaining ingredients specified. If it does not froth, the yeast is dead and should not be used. Some recipes, usually those enriched with fat and sugar, require the yeast mixture and all the liquid to be beaten with a small proportion of the flour to a yeasty batter, called the starter, and left in a warm place until it 'sponges'. Then the rest of the flour is added and the mixing completed. This method used to be common to all breads. The process takes longer but is said by old-fashioned bakers to produce the lightest, most even-textured bread.

2. Kneading, or manipulating, the dough, is the next stage. It is necessary in order to distribute the yeast cells evenly and promote the dough's elasticity. The length of the time for kneading varies according to the type of flour and the skill of the kneader, but the dough must lose its stickiness and become smooth, elastic and shiny – this usually takes about 15 minutes.

Techniques vary, but the most common one is to push the lump of dough down and away with the heel of the hand, then to pull it back with the fingers, slap it on the worktop and repeat the process, turning the dough slightly with each movement. Table-top electric mixers with dough hooks or robust food processors can also be used for kneading. They take less time than kneading by hand, but follow the manufacturer's instructions closely.

Once kneaded, the dough is formed into a ball and put into a lightly oiled, warm – not hot – bowl, and turned to coat it evenly with grease to prevent hardening and cracking. The bowl is covered with a piece of cling film, oiled polythene or a damp cloth, put in a warm (32°C/90°F) draught-free place and left until about 1^1/$_2$ times its original size. The dough should spring back when pressed lightly with a floured finger. The longer the rising takes the better. Too rapidly risen or over-risen bread has a coarse texture and a beery smell.

3. Knocking back is the next process. The risen dough is knocked down, or punched with the knuckles to push out air that may have formed large, unevenly shaped holes. Punched to its original size, it is then kneaded briefly to make it pliable. Extra sugar or dried fruit are usually added at this point, before the dough is shaped and put into a loaf tin or on to a baking sheet.

4. Proving is the second rising of the dough. When this is completed, the loaf will have doubled in bulk and should look the size and shape you hope the finished bread will be. Proving can be done in a slightly warmer place, about 40°C/100°F, for a shorter time, about 20 minutes, because the previous rising and further kneading will have made the dough even more elastic and it will rise more easily. With a second rising, the bread will be lighter when baked.

5. The bread will continue to rise in the oven for a short time partly because of the rising steam in the loaf and partly because the yeast keeps working until the dough reaches 60°C/140°F. Then the heat of the oven will cook the dough into a rigid shape. Called 'oven spring', this final rising is likely to push the top crust away from the body of the loaf. To avoid too much oven spring, bread is baked at a fairly high temperature to kill the yeast as quickly as possible.

6. The baked bread should be golden brown and have shrunk slightly from the sides of the tin. To make sure that the bread is done, it should be turned out on to a cloth and tapped on the underside. If it sounds hollow, it is done. If not, it should be returned to the oven, on its side, without the tin. Bread is cooled on a wire rack. After two hours, it will slice easily. Once stone cold it may be stored in a bread tin or a plastic bag. A lukewarm loaf stored in an airtight container will become soggy, if not mouldy.

SODA BREAD

Soda bread has bicarbonate of soda as a raising agent. However, in order to activate the soda an acid must be included in the ingredients. This is usually cream of tartar, which must be sifted with the bicarbonate of soda and the other dry ingredients to incorporate it thoroughly. When liquid is added to the dough, the alkali (bicarbonate of soda) and acid (cream of tartar) enter a chemical reaction and form carbonic acid gas. As soon as this is liberated the dough must go into the oven or the bread will not work and the flavour will be impaired. In some recipes the cream of tartar is replaced by sour milk or buttermilk. These doughs are the exact opposite of yeast doughs. High-speed mixing and quick, light handling are required, rather than careful mixing and vigorous kneading.

SHAPES FOR ROLLS

These shapes are made using approximately 55g/2oz made-up bread dough each. Once the dough has had its first rising, knock it back and divide into equal-sized pieces of dough. A 450g/1lb flour quantity of bread dough will make 16 rolls. Rolls have to be made and shaped quickly or the first rolls will have overproved before the last rolls have been shaped.

PLAIN ROLLS. Roll the dough on the work surface into a ball, pinching with the fingers to create a smooth surface on the underside. Turn the roll over, place on a baking sheet and press down slightly.

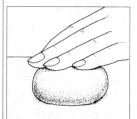

Plain roll

BAPS. As above except that when they are placed on the baking sheet press down firmly to make them round and flattish.

Bap

KNOTS. Shape the dough, with your hands, into a sausage about 10cm/4 inches long. Carefully, without stretching, tie into a knot.

Knot

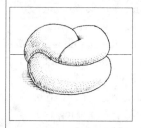

PLAITS. Divide the dough into 3 equal pieces and shape each piece into a sausage about 10cm/ 4 inches long. Put 2 pieces parallel to each other 2.5cm/1 inch apart, and put the third one across them, threading it under the left-hand piece and

over the right-hand piece. Starting from the middle take the left-hand piece and place it over the right-hand piece and proceed as for a plait (see diagrams). When one end is completed turn the plait over so that the unplaited pieces are towards you and proceed as before.

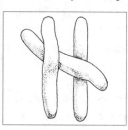

1. *Preparing to plait*
2. *Turning the plait over*
3. *The completed plait*

TWISTS OR WREATHS. Divide the dough in 2 and shape each into a sausage approximately 12cm/5 inches long. Twist each piece around the other to look like a rope, then draw round into a circle pressing the ends together.

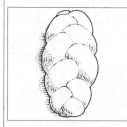

Twist

BLOOMERS. Make as for plain rolls, except oval and not round. Make 3 diagonal slashes into the surface before proving.

Bloomer

CROWNS. Shape as for plain rolls, and cut a cross into the surface before proving.

Crown

COTTAGE LOAVES. Divide the dough into 2 pieces, one three-quarters larger than the other. Shape both into balls as for plain rolls. Make a small indentation in the centre of the top of the larger one and place the smaller roll on it. Using a floured finger or a wooden spoon handle, press a hole through both rolls to the baking sheet below, thus fixing the top to the bottom.

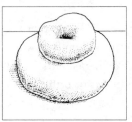

Cottage loaf

CATHERINE WHEEL. Shape the dough into a sausage approximately 15cm/6 inches long. Coil the dough round from the centre, forming a Catherine wheel.

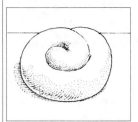

Catherine wheel

PAWNBROKER. Divide the dough into 3 equal pieces. Form each into a neat ball and place next to each other on the baking sheet to make a triangle.

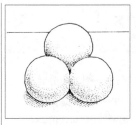

Pawnbroker

PROPELLER. Shape the dough as for plain rolls and with a pair of scissors make 1cm/^{1}/$_2$ inch snips at an angle of 45 degrees all round the edge. Prove.

Propeller

MALTESE CROSS. Shape the dough as for plain rolls and with a pair of scissors snip into the dough in 4 places as illustrated. Prove.

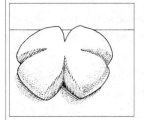

Maltese Cross

HEDGEHOGS. Shape the dough into an elongated plain roll. Pinch with finger and thumb at one end to form the nose and eyes. With a pair of scissors make tiny snips into the dough to form the prickles. Use peppercorns or currants for the eyes.

White Bread

You will need a 1 kg/2lb bread tin. If it is old and used, you may not need to grease or flour it, but if it is new and not nonstick, brush it out very lightly with flavourless oil and dust with flour.

15g/¹/₂ oz fresh yeast
290ml/¹/₂ pint lukewarm milk
5ml/1 teaspoon caster sugar
30g/1oz butter
450g/1lb plain flour (preferably 'strong')
5ml/1 teaspoon salt
1 egg, lightly beaten
egg glaze

1. Dissolve the yeast with a little of the milk and the sugar in a teacup.

2. Rub the butter into the sifted flour and salt as you would for pastry.

3. Pour in the yeast mixture, the milk and the beaten egg and mix to a softish dough.

4. Add a small amount of flour if the dough is too sticky. When the dough will leave the sides of the bowl, press it into a ball and tip it out on to a floured board.

5. Knead until it is elastic, smooth and shiny (about 15 minutes).

6. Put the dough back in the bowl and cover it with a piece of lightly greased polythene.

7. Put it somewhere warm and draught-free and leave it to rise until it has doubled in

size. This should take at least 1 hour. Bread that rises too quickly has a yeasty, unpleasant taste; the slower the rising the better – overnight in a cool larder is better than half an hour over the boiler!

8. Knead for a further 10 minutes or so.

9. Shape the dough into an oblong and put it into the loaf tin.

10. Cover with the polythene again and allow to rise again until it is the size and shape of a loaf. Brush with egg glaze.

11. Set the oven to 220°C/425°F/gas mark 7. Bake the loaf for 10 minutes, then turn the oven down to 190°C/375°F/gas mark 5 and bake for a further 25 minutes or until it is golden and firm.

12. Turn the loaf out on to a wire rack to cool. It should sound hollow when tapped on the underside. If it does not, or feels squashy and heavy, return it to the oven, without the tin, for a further 10 minutes.

NOTE: If using dried yeast or easy-blend see page 12-13.

Plaited White Loaf

450g/1lb warmed plain flour (preferably 'strong')
5ml/1 teaspoon salt
290ml/¹/₂ pint tepid milk
15g/¹/₂ oz butter
15g/¹/₂ oz fresh yeast
5ml/1 teaspoon caster sugar
1 egg, beaten
milk and poppy seeds for glazing

1. Sift the flour and salt into a warm mixing bowl. Make a well in the centre.

2. Heat the milk, melt the butter in it and allow to cool until tepid. Cream the yeast and sugar together. Mix the milk, egg and creamed yeast together and pour into the well.

3. Mix and knead until smooth and elastic (this should take 10-15 minutes). The dough should be soft.

4. Cover the bowl with a piece of oiled polythene and put to rise in a warm place for about an hour. It should double in bulk.

5. Heat the oven to 200°C/400°F/gas mark 6.

6. Divide the dough into 3 equal pieces and knead on a floured board. Form a long sausage with each piece and plait them together (see diagram, page 16). Place on a greased baking sheet.

7. Cover again with the oiled polythene and prove (allow to rise) in a warm place for 15 minutes.

8. Brush with milk, sprinkle with poppy seeds and bake for about 25 minutes or until the loaf is golden and sounds hollow when tapped on the underside.

NOTE: If using dried yeast or easy-blend see page 12-13.

Wholemeal Baps

MAKES 12 BAPS
20g/³/4 oz fresh yeast
290ml/1/2 pint lukewarm milk
5ml/1 teaspoon caster sugar
225g/8oz wholemeal flour
225g/8oz plain white flour (preferably 'strong')
5ml/1 teaspoon salt
55g/2oz butter
1 egg, lightly beaten
sesame seeds

1. Dissolve the yeast with a little of the milk and the sugar in a teacup.

2. Warm a large mixing bowl and sift the flours and salt into it. Rub in the butter as you would for pastry.

3. Pour in the yeast mixture, the milk and nearly all the beaten egg and mix to a fairly slack dough.

4. When the dough will leave the sides of the bowl, press it into a ball and tip it out on to a floured board. Knead it until it is elastic, smooth and shiny (about 15 minutes).

5. Put the dough back in the bowl and cover it with a piece of lightly greased polythene. Put it somewhere warm (on a shelf above a radiator, on the grill rack over a pan of very gently simmering water on the cooker, in the airing cupboard or just in a draught-proof corner of the kitchen). Leave it there until the dough has doubled in size. This should take at least 1 hour; the longer the better.

6. Take the dough out of the bowl, punch it down and knead it again for 10 minutes.

7. Set the oven to 200°C/400°F/gas mark 6.

8. Divide the dough into 12 pieces and shape them into flattish ovals (using a rolling pin if you like). Put on a floured baking sheet and prove (allow to rise again) for 15 minutes. Brush with the remaining beaten egg. Sprinkle with the sesame seeds.

9. Bake for 20 minutes or until firm. Leave to cool on a wire rack. Covering the baps with a tea towel will ensure a very soft crust.

NOTE: If using dried yeast or easy-blend see page 12-13.

Wholemeal Bread

This wholemeal bread is simple to make as it has only one rising. As with all bread made from purely 100% wholemeal flour it will be heavier than bread made from a mixture of flours. The flour and water quantities are approximations as wholemeal flours vary enormously. The dough should be moist but not sticky. Use the smaller quantity called for and then add extra flour or water as necessary.

550g-600g/1lb 4oz-1lb 6oz stoneground 100%
  wholemeal flour
290-340ml/10-12 fl oz warm water
45ml/3 tablespoons buttermilk
15g/$^{1}/_{2}$ oz fresh yeast (for dried yeast halve this
  quantity)
5ml/ 1 teaspoon salt

1. Warm the flour with the salt in a mixing bowl in the bottom of a low oven for about 5 minutes. Warm 2 x 675g/1$^{1}/_{2}$ lb nonstick loaf tins.

2. Mix the buttermilk with the warm water. Add a little of the liquid to the yeast with a pinch of flour. If using dried yeast, set the mixture aside to sponge for 10 minutes. It is ready when it is frothy.

3. Make a well in the centre of the flour, pour in the yeast mixture and nearly all the water and buttermilk. Mix to a dough. Add extra flour or liquid as required. Knead well.

4. Fill the warmed tins three-quarters full of dough. Smooth the tops and cover with a piece of greased polythene. Leave in a warm place for 45 minutes or until the dough has risen to the top of the tins.

5. While the dough is rising, preheat the oven to 225°C/450°F/gas mark 8.

6. Bake the bread for 15 minutes. Reduce the heat to 195°C/375°F/gas mark 5 and bake for a further 25 minutes.

7. The bread should sound hollow when it is tapped on the underside. If it does not or feels squashy and heavy, then return to the oven, without the tin, for a further 5-10 minutes. Leave to cool on a wire rack.

Brown Soda Bread

Many soda bread recipes call for buttermilk, but we have found that it works well using milk.

900g/2lb wholemeal flour, or 675g/1¹/₂lb
   wholemeal flour and 225g/8oz plain white
   flour
10ml/2 teaspoons salt
10ml/2 teaspoons bicarbonate of soda
20ml/4 teaspoons cream of tartar
10ml/2 teaspoons sugar
45g/1¹/₂ oz butter
570-860ml/1-1¹/₂ pints milk (if using all
   wholemeal flour, the recipe will need more
   liquid than if made with a mixture of 2 flours)

1. Set the oven to 190°C/375°F/gas mark 5.

2. Sift the dry ingredients into a warm dry bowl.

3. Rub in the butter and mix to a soft dough with the milk.

4. Shape with a minimum of kneading into a large circle about 5cm/2 inches thick. With the handle of a wooden spoon, make a cross on the top of the loaf. The dent should be 2cm/³/₄ inch deep.

5. Bake on a greased baking sheet for 25-30 minutes. Allow to cool on a wire rack.

Ballymaloe Brown Bread

30g/1oz yeast
5ml/1 teaspoon black treacle
350-425g/12-15 fl oz water at blood heat
450g/1lb wholemeal flour
5ml/1 teaspoon salt
15ml/1 tablespoon sesame seeds

1. Grease a 13 x 20cm/5 x 8 inch loaf tin. Mix the yeast with the treacle and 150ml/¹/₄ pint of the water, and leave in a warm place for about 5 minutes, by which time it should look creamy and slightly frothy on top.

2. Sift the flour and salt into a large bowl. Make a well in the centre and add the yeast mixture and enough of the remaining liquid to make a wettish dough that would be just too wet to knead.

3. Put the dough in the loaf tin and smooth down the surface. Sprinkle with the sesame seeds and pat down. Place the tin in a warm place and cover with a dry tea towel. Leave to rise for 15-30 minutes.

4. Preheat the oven to 230°C/470°F/gas mark 9. Then place the bread in the hot oven for 45-50 minutes. After about 30 minutes, remove the bread from the tin and replace it in the oven to continue cooking. When cooked, it should sound hollow when tapped on the bottom.

NOTE: If using dried or easy-blend yeast see page 12-13.

Beer Bread

55g/2oz butter
20ml/1 dessertspoon soft brown sugar
290ml/¹/₂ pint brown ale
30g/1oz fresh yeast
5ml/1 teaspoon salt
1 egg
225g/8oz wholewheat flour
225g/8oz plain white flour (preferably 'strong')

1. Use a little of the butter to brush out a 1kg/2lb loaf tin.

2. Bring the sugar, beer and the rest of the butter to boiling point, then allow to cool until lukewarm.

3. Use 1-2 spoons of this liquid to cream the yeast. Add the creamed yeast, salt and lightly beaten egg to the beer mixture.

4. Warm a large mixing bowl and sift the flours into it. Make a well in the centre and pour in the liquid. Mix, first with a knife, and then with your fingers, to a soft but not sloppy dough. Knead for 10 minutes or until smooth and a little shiny. The dough should be very elastic.

5. Put the dough back in the bowl and cover it with a piece of greased polythene. Put in a warm place until it has doubled in bulk.

6. Take out, punch down and knead until smooth again. Shape the dough into a loaf shape and put into the tin. Cover with the greased polythene again and put back in the warm place to prove (rise again to double its bulk). It should now look the shape of the finished loaf.

7. While it is proving, heat the oven to 200°C/400°F/gas mark 6. Bake the loaf in the middle of the oven for 35 minutes or until it is brown on top and the bread sounds hollow when tapped on the underside. Cool on a wire rack.

NOTE: If using dried yeast or easy-blend, see page 12-13.

Raisin Bread

225g/8oz black grapes, deseeded
110g/4oz raisins
85ml/3 fl oz sweet white wine
30g/1oz fresh yeast
140ml/5 fl oz warm milk
310g/11oz flour
pinch of salt
130g/5oz sugar

1. Preheat the oven to 180°C/350°F/gas mark 4.

2. Soak the grapes and raisins in the white wine.

3. Dissolve the yeast in some of the warm milk.

4. Sift the flour with the salt. Add 110g/4oz of the sugar. Make a well in the centre and add the yeast mixture and enough warm milk to make a soft but not sticky dough.

5. Knead for 5 minutes or until the dough is smooth and springy. Put in a clean bowl, covered, in a warm place, to rise for 1 hour or until double its original size.

6. Knock down the dough and re-knead for 2 minutes. Cut the dough in half and shape into 2 x 20cm/8 inch circles. Place one on a floured baking sheet and cover with three-quarters of the soaked grapes and raisins. Cover with the second piece of dough and place the remaining grapes and raisins on top. Leave covered, in a warm place, until 1¹/₂ times its original size.

7. Sprinkle with the remaining sugar and bake in the preheated oven for about 45 minutes or until the loaf is risen and brown and sounds hollow when tapped underneath.

Blue Poppy Seed and Fresh Mint Bread

675g/1¹/₂lb wholemeal flour
5ml/1 teaspoon salt
110g/4oz blue poppy seeds
45ml/3 tablespoons roughly chopped mint
55g/2oz fresh yeast
5ml/1 teaspoon muscavado sugar
570ml/1 pint lukewarm water
15ml/1 tablespoon oil

1. Sift the flour and the salt into a large mixing bowl. Stir in the poppy seeds and chopped mint and make a well in the centre.

2. Cream the yeast and sugar together. Mix the oil with the lukewarm water.

3. Put the yeast mixture and the water and oil into the well and mix with a round-bladed knife until a soft, pliable dough is obtained, adding more water if necessary.

4. When the dough will leave the sides of the bowl, press it together into a ball and tip it out on to a lightly floured work surface.

5. Knead it until it is smooth and elastic (about 10 minutes).

6. Put the dough back into the bowl, which has been washed and lightly oiled, and cover it with a piece of lightly oiled cling film. Leave the dough to rise in a warm place until it has approximately doubled in size. This should take at least 1 hour.

7. Turn the dough out on to the floured work surface, punch it down and knead for a further 10 minutes or so until it is smooth.

8. Shape the dough into an oval, place on a floured baking sheet and leave to rise again for about 15 minutes covered with the oiled cling film. Set the oven to 220°C/425°F/gas mark 7.

9. Dust the top of the loaf with a little flour and bake for 20 minutes. Turn the oven down to 190°C/375°F/gas mark 5 and bake the loaf for a further 20 minutes or until it is brown and sounds hollow when tapped on the underside.

10. Leave the loaf to cool on a wire rack.

NOTE: If using dried or easy-blend yeast see page 12-13.

Potato Bread

*450g/1lb potatoes, peeled, cooked and mashed
   with 150ml/¹/₄ pint milk and a knob of butter*
30g/1oz yeast
425ml/³/₄ pint lukewarm water
675g/1¹/₂lb flour, preferably 'strong'
10ml/2 teaspoons salt

1. Allow the potatoes to cool until lukewarm.

2. Dissolve the yeast in the lukewarm water. Mix it with the mashed potatoes.

3. Sift the flour into a bowl with the salt. Add the potato and yeast mixture and mix well. When the mixture will leave the sides of the bowl, press it into a ball and tip it out on to a floured surface.

4. Knead until it is elastic, smooth and shiny; this will probably take 15 minutes.

5. Put the dough back in the bowl and cover it with a piece of lightly greased polythene.

6. Put it somewhere warm and draught-free and leave it to rise until it has doubled in size. This should take at least 1 hour.

7. Knead for a further 10 minutes or so.

8. Shape into 3 loaves, cover with polythene and leave to prove (rise again) for 15 minutes. Dust lightly with flour.

9. Set the oven to 220°C/425°F/gas mark 7.

Bake the loaves for 10 minutes. Turn the oven down to 190°C/375°F/gas mark 5 and bake for a further 25 minutes or until golden brown and firm.

10. Turn out on to a wire rack to cool. The bread should sound hollow when tapped on the underside. If not, return to the oven for a further few minutes.

NOTE I: This recipe can be used for making attractive bread rolls. For details of making bread rolls see page 16.

NOTE II: If using dried yeast or easy-blend see page 12-13.

Cheese and Caraway Bread

675g/1¹/2lb wholemeal flour
5ml/1 teaspoon salt
30ml/2 tablespoons caraway seeds
170g/6oz Cheddar cheese, finely grated
55g/2oz fresh yeast
5ml/1 teaspoon muscavado sugar
15ml/1 tablespoon oil
570ml/1 pint lukewarm water
milk to glaze

For the topping:
30g/1oz grated cheese
15ml/1 tablespoon caraway seeds

1. Sift the flour and the salt into a large mixing bowl. Stir in the caraway seeds and grated cheese and make a well in the centre.

2. Cream the yeast and sugar together until liquid and mix the oil with the lukewarm water.

3. Put the liquid ingredients into the well, and mix with a round-bladed knife until a soft, pliable dough is obtained, adding more water if necessary.

4. When the dough will leave the sides of the bowl, press it together into a ball and tip it out on to a lightly floured surface.

5. Knead it until it is smooth and elastic (about 10 minutes).

6. Put the dough back into the bowl, which has been washed and lightly oiled, and cover it with lightly oiled cling film. Leave the dough to rise in a warm place until it has approximately doubled in size. This should take at least 1 hour.

7. Turn the dough out on to the floured surface, punch it down and knead for a further 10 minutes or so until smooth.

8. Shape the dough into a large circle, place it on a floured baking sheet, cover with the oiled cling film and leave to rise for about 15 minutes. Set the oven to 220°C/425°F/gas mark 7.

9. Brush the loaf with milk and sprinkle on the topping of grated cheese and caraway seeds. Bake it for 20 minutes and then turn the oven down to 190°C/375°F/gas mark 5. Continue baking for a further 30 minutes or until the loaf is brown and sounds hollow when it is tapped on the underside.

10. Leave the loaf to cool on a wire rack.

Cheese Gannet

15g/¹/₂ oz fresh yeast
1.5ml/¹/₃ teaspoon sugar
225g/8oz wholemeal flour
5ml/1 teaspoon salt
55g/2oz butter
105ml/3 fl oz milk
2 eggs, beaten
110g/4oz cheese, grated, preferably strong
  Cheddar or Gruyère
pinch of cayenne
pinch of English mustard
freshly ground black pepper
a little milk for glazing

1. Cream the yeast with the sugar and leave for 10 minutes.

2. Sift the flour with the salt into a warmed bowl.

3. Melt the butter in the milk and, when at blood heat, mix with the eggs and the creamed yeast. Pour this liquid into the flour and mix to a soft dough.

4. Cover and leave to rise in a warm place (do not worry if it does not rise very much – it will when cooking).

5. Set the oven to 220°C/425°F/gas mark 7.

6. Mix three-quarters of the cheese into the dough and season well with cayenne, mustard and pepper.

7. Pile into a well-greased 20cm/8 inch sandwich tin and flatten so that the mixture is about 2.5cm/1 inch deep.

Put back in the warm place to prove (rise again) for 10-15 minutes.

8. Bake in a hot oven for 35-40 minutes.

9. Five minutes before the end of cooking, brush lightly with the milk and sprinkle with the remaining cheese.

NOTE I: The mixture can be divided into 6 round rolls: put 5 around the edge of a Victoria sandwich tin and one in the middle. Leave to prove and then bake. It will look like a crown loaf.

NOTE II: If using dried yeast or easy-blend see page 12-13.

Grissini

This recipe has been taken from Arabella Boxer's *Mediterranean Cookbook*.

7g/¹/₄ oz fresh yeast
10ml/2 teaspoons sugar
45ml/3 tablespoons warm water
5ml/1 teaspoon sea salt
150ml/¹/₄ pint boiling water
225g/8oz strong flour
15ml/1 tablespoon olive oil
1 egg, beaten
55g/2oz sesame seeds

1. Set the oven to 150°C/300°F/gas mark 2.

2. Dissolve the yeast and sugar in the lukewarm water. Then dissolve the sea salt in the boiling water, allow to cool to blood temperature and then mix with the yeast.

3. Sift the flour into a large bowl, make a well in the centre, pour in the yeast mixture and the oil. Mix to a soft dough.

4. Tip the dough on to a floured board and knead for 3-4 minutes, until smooth and elastic. Cover with a damp cloth and leave for 5 minutes. Knead for 3 minutes and then divide into 20 equal pieces.

5. Roll each piece of dough out until it is as thick as your little finger. Place on oiled baking sheets and prove (allow to rise again) for 10-15 minutes.

6. Brush with beaten egg, sprinkle with sesame seeds and bake for about 45 minutes until crisp and golden brown.

Italian Bread

This is a basic olive oil bread which can be adapted easily by adding a variety of herbs such as rosemary or sage or by adding grated cheese.

30g/1oz fresh yeast
225ml/8 fl oz warm water
450g/1lb strong plain flour
10ml/2 teaspoons salt
30ml/2 tablespoons olive oil

1. Dissolve the yeast in the warm water.

2. Sift the flour and salt on to a work surface, and make a well in the centre. Pour in the dissolved yeast and olive oil. Gradually draw in the flour and when all the ingredients are well mixed, knead the dough for 8 minutes.

3. Put the dough in a lightly floured bowl. Cover with a damp tea towel and leave to rise in a warm place. This will take about 1 hour.

4. Knock back, knead lightly and shape as required, and prove for 15 minutes, or until 1¹/₂ times its original size (covered with oiled cling film). Bake at 230°C/450°F/gas mark 8 for 10 minutes. Reduce the oven to 190°C/375°F/gas mark 5 and bake for about 45 minutes. Remove to a cooling rack and leave to get completely cold.

NOTE: If using dried yeast or easy-blend see page 12-13.

Chelsea Buns

MAKES 12
15g/¹/2 oz fresh yeast
85g/3oz caster sugar
450g/1lb plain flour (preferably 'strong')
5ml/1 teaspoon salt
85g/3oz butter
1 egg
225ml/7¹/2 fl oz tepid milk
2.5ml/¹/2 teaspoon mixed spice
55g/2oz sultanas
55g/2oz currants
apricot glaze (see page 153)

1. Cream the yeast with 5ml/1 teaspoon of sugar.

2. Sift the flour into a warm dry bowl with the salt. Rub in half the butter and stir in half the sugar.

3. Beat the egg and add to the yeast mixture with the tepid milk.

4. Make a well in the centre of the flour and pour in the liquid. Using first a knife and then your hand, gradually draw the flour in from the sides of the bowl and knead until smooth.

5. Cover the bowl and leave to rise in a warm place until doubled in bulk (about 1 hour).

6. Punch the dough down again and knead again on a floured board. Roll into a square about 23cm/9 inches across.

7. Mix the remaining butter with half the remaining sugar and spread over bun mixture.

8. Sprinkle the remaining sugar, spice and fruit over the butter and sugar mixture. Set the oven to 220°C/425°F/gas mark 7.

9. Roll it up like a Swiss roll and cut into 3.5cm/1¹/2 inch slices.

10. Arrange the buns cut side up on the baking sheet and leave to prove for 15 minutes.

11. Sprinkle with sugar. Bake for 20-25 minutes. Brush with apricot glaze.

12. Leave the buns to cool on a wire rack before separating.

Hot Cross Buns

MAKES 12

20g/³/4 oz fresh yeast
55g/2oz caster sugar
220ml/7 fl oz milk
2 eggs, beaten
450g/1lb plain flour (preferably 'strong')
2.5ml/¹/2 teaspoon salt
7.5ml/¹/2 tablespoon mixed spice
85g/3oz butter
170g/6oz currants
30g/1oz finely chopped peel
a little sweetened milk for glazing

1. Cream the yeast with 5ml/1 teaspoon of the sugar.

2. Warm the milk to blood heat. Mix about two-thirds of the milk, the beaten eggs and the yeast.

3. Sift the flour, salt and spice into a mixing bowl. Rub in the butter, and add the remaining sugar. Make a well in the centre of the flour. Tip in the warm milk mixture and beat until smooth, adding more milk if necessary to produce a soft, sticky dough.

4. Turn the dough on to a floured board. Knead until the dough is very elastic.

5. Place in a lightly oiled bowl. Sprinkle with flour. Cover with a damp tea towel or an oiled sheet of polythene. Leave to rise in a warm place for about 1¹/2 hours until doubled in bulk.

6. Set the oven to 200°C/400°F/gas mark 6.

7. Turn out on to a floured board again and knock down. Knead again for a few minutes, then work in the currants and peel, making sure that they are distributed evenly.

8. Shape into small round buns. Mark a cross on top of each bun with a knife. Place on baking trays and leave to prove for approximately 15 minutes or until doubled in bulk. Brush the tops with sweetened milk.

9. Bake for about 15 minutes. Brush again with sweetened milk, bake for 2 minutes more, then cool on a wire rack.

NOTE I: The crosses can be made by laying strips of shortcrust pastry or by piping a cross of flour and water paste on top of the buns just before baking.

NOTE II: If using dried yeast or easy-blend see page 12-13.

Croissants

This recipe has been taken from the Roux Brothers' book on pâtisserie. We have tried literally dozens of croissant recipes and this is the first one we have found that works well.

The dough for croissants should be made 10-12 hours in advance. You will need a template to make the croissants. It should be an isosceles triangle 15 x 18cm/6 x 7 inches.

MAKES 16-18
45g/1¹/₂oz sugar
10g/1¹/₂ teaspoons salt
300ml/11 fl oz cold water
15g/¹/₂oz fresh yeast
30g/1oz milk powder
500g/1lb 2oz strong flour
280g/10oz butter
1 egg yolk beaten with 15ml/1 tablespoon milk
  to glaze

1. Dissolve the sugar and salt in one-third of the cold water. In a separate bowl, beat the yeast into the remaining water, then beat in the milk powder.

2. Sift the flour into a bowl and, with one hand, mix in both the liquids. Mix to a smooth soft dough but do not knead.

3. Cover the dough and leave to rise in a warm place for about 30 minutes. The dough should double in size.

4. Knock back the dough by quickly flicking it over with your fingers to release the carbon gases – do not overwork.

Cover with polythene and place in the refrigerator for 6-8 hours.

5. Shape the dough into a ball and cut a cross in the top. Roll out the dough at the 4 quarters so that it looks like 4 large 'ears' surrounding a small head.

6. Put the butter in the centre and fold the 'ears' over, ensuring that the butter is completely enclosed and will not ooze out.

7. Lightly flour the table and then carefully roll the dough away from you into a rectangle 40 x 70cm/16 x 27 inches. Brush off the excess flour and fold the dough into 3. Wrap in polythene and refrigerate for 20 minutes.

8. Repeat the rolling, folding and chilling (as in step 7) at least twice more until the dough is no longer streaky.

9. Preheat the oven to 225°C/425°F/gas mark 7.

10. Roll out the dough to a 40 x 76cm/16 x 30 inch rectangle, flouring the surface lightly and flapping up the dough occasionally to aerate it.

11. With a large knife, trim the edges and cut the dough lengthways into 2 equal strips.

12. Lay one short edge of the triangular template along one long edge of the dough and mark out the outline with the back of a knife. Invert the triangle and mark out as before. Once all the triangles are marked out (16-18 in all), cut them with a sharp knife.

13. Arrange the triangles on a baking sheet, cover tightly with polythene and then refrigerate for a few moments. If the dough becomes too warm, it may soften and crack.

14. Place the triangles, one at a time, on the work surface with the long point towards you. Stretch out the 2 shorter points and begin to roll the triangle towards you. Make sure that the central point is in the middle and underneath so that it does not rise up during cooking.

15. As soon as they are shaped, place the croissants on a baking sheet, turning in the corners to make a crescent shape. Since the sides of the oven are the hottest, the last row of croissants must face inwards or the points may dry out or burn.

16. Lightly brush the croissants with egg wash, working from the inside outwards so that the layers of dough do not stick together. Leave to rise in a warm draught-free place until they have doubled in size.

17. Lightly re-glaze the croissants with egg wash. Bake the croissants in the preheated oven for 15 minutes. Transfer to a wire rack to cool.

NOTE: If using dried or easy-blend yeast see page 12-13.

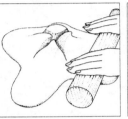
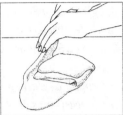

Steps 5 and 6 in the text

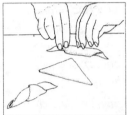

Steps 12 and 14 in the text

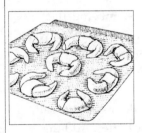

The finished croissants

Stollen

450g/1lb strong white flour
5ml/1 teaspoon caster sugar
15g/¹/₂ oz fresh yeast, or 1¹/₂ teaspoons
*   dried yeast*
250ml/8 fl oz warm milk
5ml/1 teaspoon salt
85g/3oz butter
110g/4oz currants
110g/4oz sultanas
30g/1oz chopped mixed peel
30g/1oz walnuts or almonds, chopped
10ml/2 teaspoons grated orange or lemon rind
1 egg
55g/2oz glacé cherries
icing sugar for dusting

1. Prepare a yeast batter: mix together 110g/4oz flour, the sugar, yeast and warm milk. Set aside until bubbly. This will take about 20 minutes in a warm place.

2. Mix the remaining flour with the salt. Rub in 55g/2oz of the butter. Add the currants, sultanas, mixed peel, nuts and citrus rind.

3. Beat the egg, add it to the yeast batter with the flour, fruit and nuts. Mix well to a soft but not too sticky dough.

4. Knead until smooth and elastic. This will take about 10 minutes. Shape into a ball and leave in a warm place in a clean bowl covered with cling wrap or in a polythene bag, until doubled in bulk. This will take at least 1 hour. The dried fruits and nuts slow down the rising and proving of a bread dough.

5. Knead again (knock down) for 2 minutes and shape into an oval 30 x 20cm/12 x 8 inches.

6. Melt the remaining butter and brush half of it over the bread dough. Spread the glacé cherries over half the dough. Fold the other half over the dough and press down lightly. Cover with greased polythene and leave to prove until 1¹/₂ times its original size – this may take between 15 minutes and half an hour.

7. Set the oven to 190°C/375°F/gas mark 5.

8. Brush the remaining butter over the proved loaf and bake for 20-25 minutes. Leave to cool on a wire rack. Dust with icing sugar.

NOTE: An alternative version is to use 225g/8oz made-up marzipan to stuff the stollen in place of the cherries and butter. Roll the marzipan into a sausage and place in the middle of the dough. Roll up and seal the ends by pinching them together. Bake as before.

Brioche

MAKES 12 SMALL BRIOCHES OR 1
LARGE ONE
25ml/5 level teaspoons caster sugar
30ml/2 tablespoons warm water
225g/8oz flour
pinch of salt
2 eggs, beaten
55g/2oz melted butter, cool
7g/¹/₄oz fresh yeast

For the glaze:
1 egg mixed with 15ml/1 tablespoon water and
   15ml/1 teaspoon sugar

1. Grease a large brioche mould or 12 small
brioche tins.

2. Mix the yeast with 5ml/1 teaspoon of
the sugar and the water. Leave to dissolve.

3. Sift the flour with a pinch of salt into a
bowl. Sprinkle over the sugar. Make a well
in the centre. Drop in the eggs, yeast
mixture and melted butter and mix with
the fingers of one hand to a soft but not
sloppy paste. Knead on an unfloured board
for 5 minutes or until smooth. Put into a
clean bowl, cover with a damp cloth or
greased polythene and leave to rise in a
warm place until doubled in bulk (about 1
hour).

4. Turn out and knead again on an
unfloured board for 2 minutes.

5. Place the dough in the brioche mould (it
should not come more than halfway up the
mould). If making individual brioches,
divide the dough into 12 pieces. Using
three-quarters of each piece, roll them into
small balls and put them in the brioche
tins. Make a dip on top of each brioche.
Roll the remaining paste into 12 tiny balls
and press them into the prepared holes.
Push a pencil, or thin spoon handle, right
through each small ball into the brioche
base as this will anchor the balls in place
when baking.

6. Cover with greased polythene and leave
in a warm place until risen to the top of the
tin(s). The individual ones will take 15
minutes, the large one about 30 minutes.

7. Set the oven to 200°C/400°F/gas mark 6.

8. Brush the egg glaze over the brioches.
Bake the large one for 20-25 minutes, or
small ones for 10 minutes

NOTE: If using dried yeast or easy-blend
see page 12-13.

Cakes, Scones, Buns and Biscuits

Cake-Making

SUCCESSFUL cake-making is a most satisfying activity for the cook. It is also most demanding on account of the accuracy needed in measuring the ingredients and the skill necessary in preparing certain cakes. Confidence is best built by beginning with the easier cakes, such as gingerbread or fruit cake. The first attempts at making more difficult cakes such as a génoise sponge are often disappointing. Happily, practice, with good ingredients, proper utensils, careful weighing and measuring, precise oven temperatures and exact timing – in short, careful attention to detail – makes perfect.

Most cakes are made by mixing fat, sugar, flour, eggs and liquid. Air or another gas is incorporated to make the mixture rise during baking. As it bakes, strands of gluten in the flour are stretched by the gas given off until the heat finally hardens the cake. It is even rising that gives a cake a light sponge-like texture.

INGREDIENTS

FATS. Butter makes the best flavoured cakes. Margarine, particularly the soft or 'tub' variety, is useful for speed but has less flavour than butter. Vegetable shortenings are flavourless but give light cakes. Lard cakes are often delicious but heavy, and for this reason lard is little used in cake-making. Oils are not much used as they do not easily hold air when they are creamed or beaten, and the resulting cakes can therefore be heavy.

SUGARS. The finer creaming possible with caster (fine granulated) sugar makes it most suitable for cake-making. Very coarse granulated sugar can give a speckled appearance to a finished cake unless the sugar is ground down first in a blender or food processor. Soft brown sugars give colour and flavour to dark cakes like gingerbread, but they give sponge cakes a drab look and too much caramel flavour.

Golden syrup, honey, treacle and molasses are used in cakes made by the melting method. Such cakes are cooked relatively slowly, as these thick liquid sugars tend to caramelize and burn at higher temperatures.

EGGS. Unless specified, most recipes assume a medium-sized egg weighing 55/2oz (UK size 3). The eggs should be used at room temperature – cold eggs tend to curdle the mixture and this results in the cake having a tough, coarse, too open texture. When using whisked egg whites in a cake, be sure not to allow even a speck of yolk into the whites. Any yolk or fat on the whisk will prevent proper whisking of the whites, reducing their air-holding ability and the lightness of the finished cake.

FLOURS. Plain white flour is used in cake making unless otherwise specified. The high proportion of 'soft' or low-gluten wheat used in European plain flour makes it particularly suitable for cake-making. In North America, plain or 'all-purpose' flour is made with more 'hard' than soft wheat, so cornflour, which is also weak (low in gluten), is sometimes substituted for some of the all-purpose flour, or special soft 'cake flour' is used. Although a little gluten is needed to allow the mixture to stretch and expand as it rises, too much would give a tough, chewy cake.

Self-raising flour has a raising agent (baking powder) added to it and should be used only if specified in the recipe. All flours, even if labelled 'ready-sifted', should be sifted before use to eliminate any lumps and to incorporate air.

RAISING AGENTS

AIR is incorporated into cake mixtures by agitating the ingredients. Methods include sifting the flour, beating the butter and beating or creaming it again with the sugar to a fluffy, mousse-like consistency, and whisking the eggs. The heat of the oven causes the air trapped in the mixture to rise and leaven or lighten the cake, either by itself or in conjunction with other raising agents.

STEAM raises some mixtures even when air has not been beaten into them. Flour mixtures with a high proportion of liquid in them, like Yorkshire pudding, will rise in a hot oven since, as the water vaporizes and the steam rises, the uncooked flour mixture rises with it. While in this puffed-up state, the mixture hardens in the oven heat with the steam trapped inside. The pockets of air created by steam are uneven and very open, as in choux pastry (see page 97), so steam is not used on its own for making cakes. But steam is a contributing factor in raising wet cake mixtures such as gingerbread.

BICARBONATE OF SODA, or *BAKING SODA,* is a powder which, when mixed into cake mixtures, quickly gives off half its substance as carbon dioxide. In a cake the trapped gas causes the mixture to puff up. Heat sets the mixture once it has risen. By the time the cake cools, the gas will have escaped and will have been replaced by air. Unfortunately, the bicarbonate of soda remaining in the cake can give it a slightly unpleasant smell and taste, and a yellowish colour. For this reason, bicarbonate of soda is most often used in strong-tasting cakes such as gingerbread and those flavoured with chocolate, treacle or molasses. The carbon dioxide reaction is speeded up by acidic substances, so bicarbonate of soda is usually used in cake mixtures with ingredients such as sour milk, vinegar, buttermilk, soured cream, cream of tartar or yoghurt. This makes it especially suitable for quickly mixed items like fruit cakes, scones, soda bread and gingerbread. It also gives them a soft texture and spongy crust with a deep colour. Unfortunately, the process destroys some of the vitamins present in the flour.

BAKING POWDER in commercial forms consists of bicarbonate of soda and an acid powder that varies according to the brand, plus a starch filler, usually cornflour, arrowroot or ground rice. The starch keeps the mixture dry by absorbing any dampness in the air, which might cause the soda and the acid in the powder to react. The presence of the filler explains why more commercial baking powder than mixed 'bi-carb' and cream of tartar would be needed to raise the same cake. A 'delayed action' or 'double action' baking powder is sold in the USA that needs heat as well as moisture to produce carbon dioxide. It is not widely known in Europe. The advantage of it is that it can be added to mixtures in advance of baking – it starts to work only once in the oven.

YEAST cakes caused to rise by the growth of yeast cells are really sweetened enriched breads. They are traditional in East European cookery. The kulich on page 62 is a classic example.

PREPARING A CAKE TIN

All tins should be greased before use to prevent the cake mixture from sticking or burning at the edges or bottom. Melted lard or oil are the most suitable fats. Always turn the tin upside down after greasing to allow any excess fat to drain away. Use a paint brush to get a thin layer. Bread tins and nonstick sandwich tins need no preparation other than greasing. Tins for cakes made by the melting or creaming methods should be greased, then the base lined with greaseproof paper, cut exactly to size and the paper brushed out with more melted lard or oil. (To cut the paper accurately draw round the tin, then cut just inside the line). For cakes made by the whisking method, a dusting of caster sugar and flour should be given after lining and greasing.

For fruit cakes, grease the tin, then line the sides and base with greaseproof paper as follows:
1. Cut 2 pieces of greaseproof paper to fit the base of the cake tin.
2. Cut another piece long enough to go right round the sides of the tin and to overlap slightly. It should be 2.5cm/1 inch deeper than the height of the cake tin.
3. Fold one long edge of this strip over 2.5cm/1 inch all along its length.
4. Cut snips at right angles to the edge and about 1cm/^{1}/2 inch apart, all along the folded side. The snips should just reach the fold.
5. Grease the tin, place one paper base in the bottom and grease again.
6. Fit the long strip inside the tin with the folded cut edge on the bottom (the flanges will overlap slightly) and the main uncut part lining the sides of the tin. Press them well into the corners.
7. Grease the paper and lay the second base on top of the first.
8. Brush the base again with more melted lard or oil and dust the lined pan with flour.

METHODS USED IN CAKE-MAKING

RUBBING IN. The rubbing-in method gives a fairly substantial cake (such as rock cakes) with a crumbly moist texture. The raising agent is always bicarbonate of soda. In rock cakes the agent is in the self-raising flour. The cake is delicious served sliced and spread with butter, or eaten as a warm pudding with custard.

MELTING. The melting method is used for very moist cakes like gingerbread. The fat, sugar, syrup and any other liquid ingredients are heated together to melt, then cooled slightly. The flour and other dry ingredients are sifted together and the warm sugar mixture is stirred, not beaten, into the dry mixture along with the eggs. The raising agent is always bicarbonate of soda. These cakes are the perfect cake for the beginner – easy, reliable and delicious.

CLASSIC CREAMING. Creaming fat and sugar to a mousse-like consistency, and thereby incorporating air, is the secret of lightness in cakes like the Victoria sponge, although a little chemical raising agent is usually added to ensure rising. First the butter or margarine is creamed or beaten until it is smooth and very light in colour, but the fat is never allowed to melt. If it did the carefully incorporated air beaten into it would escape. The sugar is then beaten in by degrees, until the mixture is pale and fluffy.

The eggs are lightly beaten and added, also by degrees, to the creamed mixture. The mix is beaten after each addition to thoroughly incorporate it. At this point the batter can curdle, especially if the eggs are too cold, but beating in 15ml/1 tablespoon of sifted flour taken from the recipe after each addition of eggs should prevent this. Cakes made from curdled mixtures are acceptable, but they have a less delicate, more open and coarse texture than those made from uncurdled mixture.

Plain flour, if used, should be sifted with the baking powder and salt. Self-raising flour should be sifted with salt. The flour mixture is then folded carefully into the creamed mixture with a metal spoon and with as little mixing as possible to ensure minimum air loss in the batter.

ALL-IN-ONE CREAMING. The all-in-one method is an easy version of the creaming method, because all the ingredients are beaten together at the same time, but a strong electric mixer is necessary to make these cakes really successful. Soft 'tub' margarine gives a lighter result than butter.

CREAMING FOR FRUIT CAKES. Another version of the creaming method is suited to fruit cakes. Softened butter and sugar are creamed in a mixing bowl to incorporate air. The eggs and any other liquid are gradually beaten into the creamed mixture, with the flour added with the last few additions of egg to reduce the risk of curdling. After the mixture is well combined, the dry fruit is folded in well to distribute it throughout the cake. The mixture should have a soft, dropping consistency (it should fall reluctantly off a spoon given a slight shake, neither sticking obstinately nor running off) and be spread out evenly in the prepared tin, with a slight dip in the centre of the mixture to counteract the cake 'peaking'.

Because fruit cakes are generally large and dense and contain a high proportion of fruit, which burns easily, they are cooked extremely slowly. To prevent burning they can be placed on a folded newspaper in the oven and can be covered in several layers of greaseproof or brown paper, but not foil, which traps the steam and produces too doughy a result.

WHISKING. In the whisking method, the only raising agent is air that has been trapped in the cake batter during mixing. As the air expands in the heat of the oven, the cake rises. Cakes like Swiss roll and génoise commune are made by this method.

The simplest whisked sponge contains no fat. Sugar and eggs are whisked together until they are thick and light, then flour is folded in gently to keep in as much air as possible. In a lighter but more complicated whisked sponge, the eggs are separated and the yolks are whisked with the sugar and flour. The whites are whisked in another bowl, then folded into the batter. Sometimes half the sugar is whisked with the yolks, and half with the whites to give a meringue.

The sugar and eggs (or egg yolks only) are whisked in a bowl set over a pan of barely simmering water. Make sure that the bowl does not touch the water or the heat will scramble the eggs. Gentle heat from the steam speeds up the dissolving of the sugar and slightly cooks and thickens the eggs, so encouraging the mixture to hold the maximum number of air bubbles. The mixture should change colour from yellow to almost white and increase to four times its original volume. The mixture is ready when a lifted whisk will leave a ribbon-like trail. Traditionally, a balloon whisk is used, but a hand-held electric one works excellently. If a powerful food mixer is used, the heat can be dispensed with, though the process is speeded up if the mixture is put into a warmed bowl.

When the flour is folded in, great care should be take to fold rather than stir or beat, as the aim is to incorporate the flour without losing any of the beaten-in air, which alone will raise the cake. The correct movement is more of lifting the mixture and cutting into it, rather than stirring it.

Although they are light and springy, a drawback to these cakes is that they go stale quickly. Always plan to make fatless sponge on the day of serving, or freeze the cake once it is cool.

The génoise is a whisked sponge that has just-runny butter folded into it with the flour. Butter gives it flavour and richness and makes it keep a day or two longer than fatless sponges. The butter should be poured in a stream around the edge of the bowl and then folded in. If the butter is poured heavily on top of the whisked mixture, it forces out some of the air, and needs excessive mixing, with the danger of more air loss.

Whisked cakes are cooked when the surface will spring back when pressed with a finger. The cakes should be cooled for a few minutes in the tin and then turned out on to a cake rack. The baking paper should be carefully peeled off to allow the escape of steam.

Victoria Sandwich

oil for preparing 2 x 15cm/6 inch cake tins
110g/4oz butter
110g/4oz caster sugar
2 eggs
110g/4oz self-raising flour
water
30ml/2 tablespoons raspberry jam
caster sugar

1. Set oven to 190°C/375°F/gas mark 5. Prepare the cake tins by lining the bottom of each with a disc of greaseproof paper and lightly brushing out each tin with oil.

2. Cream the butter and sugar together until light and fluffy.

3. Mix the eggs together in a separate bowl, and gradually beat into the creamed mixture a little at a time, adding 15ml/1 tablespoon of flour if the mixture begins to curdle at any stage.

4. Fold in the sifted flour, adding enough water to bring the mixture to a dropping consistency. Then divide the mixture between the tins and bake in the middle of the oven for about 20 minutes, or until the cakes are well risen, golden and feel spongy to the fingertips.

5. Allow the cakes to cool for a few minutes in the tins, then turn out on to a wire rack to cool completely.

6. Sandwich the cakes together with raspberry jam. Dust the top of the cake with caster sugar.

Madeira Cake

melted lard for greasing
170g/6oz unsalted butter
170g/6oz caster sugar
grated rind and juice of 1 lemon
pinch of ground cinnamon
3 eggs
110g/4oz self-raising flour
55g/2oz ground almonds
milk, if necessary
1 slice candied lemon (citrus peel)

1. Prepare an 18cm/7 inch cake tin (see page 40).

2. Set the oven to 170°C/325°F/gas mark 3.

3. Cream the butter and beat in the sugar until light and fluffy. Add the lemon rind and cinnamon.

4. Beat in the eggs one at a time, adding a little flour as you beat, to prevent the mixture from curdling. Add the lemon juice. Then fold in the remaining flour and the ground almonds with a metal spoon.

5. Add enough milk to bring the mixture to a dropping consistency (it should drop rather than run off a spoon).

6. Spoon the mixture into the cake tin and spread with a palette knife or spatula. Arrange the citrus peel on top of the cake. Then bake for 1¼ hours.

7. Cool the cake for 10 minutes in the tin before gently easing out on to a wire rack.

Black Bun

A rich, dense, fruity cake which is served in Scotland over the Christmas holiday, but particularly at Hogmanay. Serve in very small pieces.

For the pastry:
340g/12oz plain flour
1/2 level teaspoon baking powder
pinch of salt
55g/2oz lard
110g/4oz butter
egg glaze

For the filling:
450g/1lb currants
340g/12oz raisins
45ml/3 tablespoons whisky
55g/2oz mixed peel
55g/2oz chopped almonds
85g/3oz soft dark brown sugar
170g/6oz plain flour
2.5ml/1/2 level teaspoon baking powder
2.5ml/1/2 level teaspoon cream of tartar
5 ml/1 teaspoon ground allspice
2.5ml/1/2 teaspoon ground ginger
2.5ml/1/2 teaspoon ground cinnamon
2.5ml/1/2 teaspoon grated nutmeg
2.5ml/1/2 2 teaspoon ground black pepper
pinch of salt
290ml/1/2 pint milk

1. Grease a 900g/2lb loaf tin. Preheat the oven to 160°C/325°F/gas mark 3.

2. Make the pastry: sift the flour with the baking powder and salt. Chop the lard and butter into small pieces and rub into the flour until the mixture looks like coarse breadcrumbs. Add enough cold water to bind the pastry together.

3. Roll out three-quarters of the pastry and use to line the loaf tin. If it cracks, push it into the tin to seal. Chill in the refrigerator for 30 minutes.

4. Soak the currants and raisins in the whisky for 30 minutes. Add the mixed peel, almonds and sugar, and mix thoroughly. Sift the flour with all the other dry ingredients and stir into the fruit mixture.

5. Add the milk to bind the fruit together. Pack tightly into the prepared pastry case.

6. Roll out the remaining pastry and place on top of the fruit. Crimp the edges and glaze with egg glaze. Push a skewer right through the bun, making a hole to the base. Make 4 holes along the length of the bun, and prick the top surface all over with a fork.

7. Place in the middle of the preheated oven and bake for 3 hours. Then allow to cool before removing from the tin.

NOTE I: It is best if kept for 2 weeks before eating.

NOTE II: If this is made in a deep loaf tin, line the tin with a strip of greaseproof paper which can later be used as a handle to help lift the bun out of the tin.

Christmas Cake

110g/4oz glacé cherries
55g/2oz mixed peel
450g/1lb raisins
285g/10oz sultanas
110g/4oz currants
225g/8oz butter
225g/8oz soft brown sugar
5 eggs, beaten
285g/10oz flour
10ml/2 teaspoons mixed spice
30ml/2 tablespoons black treacle
grated lemon rind
2 wine glasses of beer or sherry (200ml/7 fl oz)
110g/4oz ground almonds

1. Set the oven to 170°C/325°F/gas mark 3 and prepare a 22cm/9 inch round cake tin (see page 40).

2. Cut up the cherries and mix with the rest of the fruit. Cream the butter until soft. Add the sugar and beat together until light and fluffy. Then add the beaten eggs slowly, beating well between each addition. If the mixture curdles, beat in 5ml/1 teaspoon of flour.

3. Fold in the flour, mixed spice, lemon rind, black treacle and beer or sherry. Stir in the ground almonds and fruit.

4. Place the mixture in the prepared tin and make a deep hollow in the middle.

5. Bake for 2^1/2 hours or until a skewer emerges clean from being stuck in the middle of the cake. Allow to cool on a wire rack.

Rice Cake

110g/4oz butter
225g/8oz caster sugar
finely grated rind of ^{1}/2 lemon
4 eggs
225g/8oz ground rice

1. Set the oven to 180°C/350°F/gas mark 4. Line an 18cm/7 inch cake tin with a double layer of greased and floured greaseproof paper.

2. Cream the butter in a mixing bowl. Beat in the sugar until light and fluffy. Add the lemon rind and mix well.

3. Separate the eggs. Add the yolks to the mixture one at a time, beating hard all the time.

4. Whisk the egg whites until fairly stiff but not dry. Take a spoonful of egg white and mix it in. Stir in half the ground rice. Add half the remaining egg white. Add the rest of the ground rice, then the rest of the egg white.

5. Pour into the tin. Make a slight hollow in the centre of the mixture to counteract any tendency to rise in the middle.

6. Bake for 45 minutes or until firm to the touch and slightly shrunken at the edges.

7. Cool in the tin for 5 minutes, then turn out on to a wire rack to cool completely.

Coffee Almond Layer Cake

110g/4oz butter
110g/4oz caster sugar
85g/3oz plain flour
pinch of salt
5ml/1 teaspoon baking powder
2 eggs
10ml/2 teaspoons instant coffee, dissolved
  in 30ml/2 tablespoons hot water
55g/2oz ground almonds

For the filling:
170g/6oz unsalted butter
340g/12oz icing sugar
10ml/2 teaspoons instant coffee powder
55g/2oz flaked toasted almonds to decorate

1. Butter 2 x 18cm/7 inch sandwich tins (see page 40). Set the oven to 190°C/375°F/gas mark 5.

2. Cream the butter and beat in the sugar until light and fluffy.

3. Sift the flour, salt and baking powder. Beat the eggs lightly.

4. Add the eggs and flour alternately by degrees to the butter and sugar mixture. Stir in the coffee and the ground almonds. Divide the mixture between the tins and smooth the tops with a spatula.

5. Bake for 20-25 minutes or until the cake is firm and golden brown. Allow to cool in the tins for 5 minutes, then turn out on to wire racks and leave until stone cold.

6. Meanwhile, make the filling: beat the butter and sugar until light and fluffy and stir in the coffee.

7. Sandwich the cake layers with half the butter icing and spread the remainder around the sides and top of the cake. Decorate with flaked almonds.

Simnel Cake

A festive Easter cake: the 11 balls of marzipan are said to represent the apostles (without Judas). Sometimes they are made into egg shapes, the symbol of spring and rebirth.

large pinch each of salt and baking powder
225g/8oz plain flour
55g/2oz rice flour
110g/4oz glacé cherries
225g/8oz butter
225g/8oz caster sugar
grated rind of 1 lemon
4 eggs, separated
225g/8oz sultanas
110g/4oz currants
30g/1oz candied peel, chopped
340g/12oz marzipan (see page 157)
beaten egg
110g/4oz glacé icing (see page 156)

1. Set the oven to 180°C/350°F/gas mark 4. Prepare a 20cm/8 inch cake tin with a double lining of greased and floured greaseproof paper. Wrap the outside of the cake tin with a double thickness of brown paper to insulate the cake from direct heat.

2. Sift the salt, baking powder and flours. Cut the cherries in half.

3. Cream the butter until soft. Add the sugar and beat until light and fluffy. Add the lemon rind.

4. Beat in the egg yolks. Whisk the whites until stiff.

5. Fold one-third of the sifted flour into the mixture. Fold in the egg whites by degrees, alternating with the remaining flour and the fruit and peel.

6. Put half the mixture into the prepared tin, spreading a little up the sides of the tin.

7. Take just over one-third of the marzipan paste. Roll it into a smooth round. Place in the cake tin. Cover with the remaining mixture.

8. With a palette knife make a dip in the centre of the cake to counteract any tendency to rise in the middle.

9. Bake for 2 hours, then reduce the oven heat to 150°C/300°F/gas mark 2. Bake for a further 30 minutes.

10. Roll the remaining marzipan into a circle the same size as the top of the cake. Cut a piece from the centre about 12.5cm/5 inches in diameter and shape into 11 small, even-sized balls.

11. Heat the grill. Lay the ring of marzipan on top of the cake and brush with egg wash. Arrange the marzipan balls on top of the ring and brush again with beaten egg. Grill until golden brown.

12. When cold pour a little glacé icing into the centre of the cake. Tie a ribbon around the side.

Chocolate and Orange Cake

For the cake:
85g/3oz dark sweetened chocolate
5ml/1 teaspoon vanilla essence
340g/12oz soft brown sugar
290ml/^{1}/2 pint milk
grated rind of ^{1}/2 orange
110g/4oz butter
2 eggs
225g/8oz plain flour
5ml/1 level teaspoon bicarbonate of soda

For the filling:
grated rind of ^{1}/2 orange
290ml/^{1}/2 pint thick cream, whipped
caster sugar to taste

For the icing:
110g/4oz dark sweetened chocolate
60ml/4 tablespoons milk

1. To make the cake set the oven to 190°C/375°F/gas mark 5. Line the bottom of 3 sandwich tins with greaseproof paper and brush them with melted lard or butter.

2. Put the chocolate, vanilla, half the sugar and half the milk into a saucepan. Cook, stirring until quite smooth. Add the grated orange rind.

3. Beat the butter with the rest of the sugar until very light and creamy. Beat in the eggs, then add the chocolate mixture and beat again. Sift in the flour and soda and beat well to get rid of all lumps. Add the rest of the milk and stir. The mixture

should now have the consistency of pancake batter.

4. Divide the mixture between the 3 cake tins and bake in the middle of the oven for about 30 minutes or until the rounds have a very slightly shrivelled look around the edges. Do not worry if they do not feel very firm – they should be very moist and rather sticky. Allow to cool for 3 minutes before turning out on to a wire rack to cool. Peel off the paper.

5. To make the filling: mix the orange rind into the whipped cream and sweeten to taste. Make a triple-deck cake with the cream filling between the 3 layers of cake.

6. To make the icing: put the chocolate and milk into a saucepan. Heat, stirring, until smooth and thick. Cool slightly and pour or spread over the top of the cake.

Chocolate Fudge Cake

110g/4oz butter
110g/4oz caster sugar
2 eggs
30ml/2 tablespoons golden syrup
30g/1oz ground almonds
110g/4oz self-raising flour
pinch of salt
30g/1oz cocoa powder

For the icing:
110g/4oz granulated sugar
110ml/4 fl oz milk
140g/5oz plain chocolate, chopped
55g/2oz butter
30ml/2 tablespoons double cream
vanilla essence

1. Preheat the oven to 180°C/350°F/gas mark 4.

2. Grease and line the base of an 18cm/7 inch diameter deep cake tin with a circle of greaseproof paper.

3. Cream the butter until soft, add the sugar. Beat until light and fluffy.

4. Whisk the eggs together and add a little at a time to the butter and sugar mixture, beating well between each addition. If the mixture curdles, beat 5ml/1 teaspoon flour into it.

5. Stir in the golden syrup and ground almonds.

6. Sift together the self-raising flour and cocoa powder and fold into the mixture.

7. The cake mixture should have a reluctant dropping consistency; if it is too thick add a little water or milk.

8. Pile the mixture into the cake tin, spread flat with a palette knife and bake for 40 minutes or until the cake is well risen and feels spongy.

9. Turn out and cool on a wire rack.

10. Meanwhile, make the icing: put the sugar and milk into a pan over a low heat. Allow the sugar to dissolve and then bring it up to the boil. Simmer, without stirring, for 8 minutes.

11. Take the pan off the heat and stir in the chocolate; add the butter, cream and vanilla essence. Stir until completely melted.

12. Put into a bowl, cover and allow to chill for 2 hours until the icing is spreadable.

13. When the cake is cool, split it in half horizontally and sandwich back together again using a quarter of the icing. Spread the remaining icing on the top and sides of the cake, swirling it to give a frosted appearance.

Old-Fashioned Boiled Christmas Cake

This cake is not, as the name suggests, boiled instead of baked, but the fruit is boiled in water and orange juice and allowed to stand for 3 days before completing. This gives the fruit a wonderful plumpness. Instead of being decorated with marzipan and icing it is finished with a glazed fruit and nut topping and a pretty ribbon.

For the cake:
225g/8oz sultanas
225g/8oz raisins
110g/4oz currants
55g/2oz mixed peel
55g/2oz glacé cherries, halved
170g/6oz dried apricots, chopped
55g/2oz dried apples, chopped
110g/4oz dried dates, chopped
110g/4oz dried peaches, chopped
110g/4oz dried pears, chopped
225g/8oz butter
225g/8oz brown sugar
grated rind and juice of 1 lemon
grated rind and juice of 1 orange
110ml/4 fl oz water
110ml/4 fl oz orange juice
110ml/4 fl oz brandy
2.5ml/1½ teaspoon grated nutmeg
5ml/1 teaspoon ground cinnamon
5ml/1 teaspoon allspice
2.5ml/1½ teaspoon ground ginger
1.25ml/1¼ teaspoon ground cardamom
15ml/1 tablespoon black treacle

5 eggs, beaten
310g/11oz plain flour
5ml/1 teaspoon baking powder

For the fruit topping:
340g/12oz mixed dried fruit and nuts, e.g. pecans, brazils, almonds, apricots, red and green cherries, prunes, peaches, pears etc.
340g/12oz apricot jam

1. Put the sultanas, raisins, currants, mixed peel, cherries, apricots, apples, dates, peaches, pears, butter, sugar, lemon and orange rind and juice, water and orange juice into a large pan.

2. Bring slowly up to the boil. Stir with a wooden spoon, cover with a lid, and simmer for 10 minutes.

3. Remove from the heat and allow to cool slightly.

4. Add the brandy and spices and transfer to a large bowl. When it is completely cold, cover and put in a cool place (not the refrigerator) for 3 days, stirring daily.

5. Prepare a 25cm/10 inch round cake tin by lining with double sheets of greaseproof paper (see page 40)

6. Preheat the oven to 170°C/325°F/gas mark 3.

7. Stir the treacle into the boiled fruit mixture and beat in the eggs. Sift together the flour and baking powder and stir into the cake mixture, which will be slightly sloppy.

8. Turn the mixture into the prepared cake tin and bake for approximately $4^1/2$ hours, or until a skewer inserted into the centre of the cake comes out clean.

9. Leave to cool in the tin.

10. When completely cold, wrap up carefully in aluminium foil until ready to decorate. It will mature well for 2-3 months.

11. To decorate the cake: put the apricot jam in a pan with 15ml/1 tablespoon of water. Heat until boiling and then push through a sieve. Allow to cool slightly and then brush the top of the cake with the apricot glaze.

12. Arrange the fruit and nuts all over the top of the cake in a haphazard fashion and then, using a pastry brush, glaze carefully with the apricot glaze.

NOTE I: The glaze will remain shiny on the cake for a few days but after a week it will begin to lose its gloss so it is better not to decorate the cake too early.

NOTE II: If the cake top becomes very dark whilst cooking cover it with a double layer of damp greaseproof paper.

Pain de Gênes (Rich Almond Cake)

110g/4oz blanched almonds
3 eggs
140g/5oz caster sugar
55g/2oz potato starch or plain flour
2.5ml/1/2 teaspoon baking powder
good pinch of salt
85g/3oz butter
15ml/1 tablespoon Amaretto or Kirsch
icing sugar

1. Set the oven at 180°C/350°F/gas mark 4.
Brush a moule-à-manqué or 20cm/8 inch
cake tin with butter, line the bottom with a
circle of greaseproof paper and brush again.

2. Grind the almonds finely. Then whisk
the eggs and sugar together until light and
fluffy.

3. Sift the flour, baking powder and salt
into a bowl. Stir into the nuts. Half fold
this into the egg and sugar mixture.
Then melt the butter and carefully fold it
into the cake mixture with the minimum of
stirring. Add the Kirsch or Amaretto.
Pour into the cake tin.

4. Bake for 30-35 minutes or until the cake
is brown on top and springs back when
lightly pressed with a finger. Then allow
the cake to cool for 5 minutes in the tin;
then loosen the sides with a knife and turn
out onto a wire rack to cool. When cold,
sift a thin layer of icing sugar over the top.

Coffee Génoise with Chocolate Caraque

For the cake:
4 large eggs
125g/41/2 oz caster sugar
55g/2oz butter, melted but cool
100g/31/2 oz plain flour
10ml/2 teaspoons coffee powder

For the coffee butter cream filling and icing:
110g/4oz sugar
150ml/1/4 pint milk
2 egg yolks
225g/8oz unsalted butter
coffee essence

For the chocolate caraque:
30g/1oz dark chocolate
browned chopped almonds for decoration
icing sugar

1. Prepare a moule-à-manqué or deep
sandwich tin (see page 40). Set the oven to
190°C/375°F/gas mark 5.

2. Break the eggs into a bowl, add the
sugar and set the bowl over a saucepan of
simmering water. Whisk until the mixture
has doubled in bulk. Whisk off the heat
until the mixture has cooled. (If using an
electric mixer, beating need not be done
over heat.) Quickly whisk in the butter – if
you work too slowly the cake will collapse.
Then sift the flour and coffee powder over
the cake mixture and fold it in thoroughly
but gently with a large metal spoon.

Turn into the prepared cake tin.

3. Bake for about 35 minutes or until cooked – the edges should look slightly shrivelled. Allow to cool slightly in the tin and then turn out on to a wire rack. Peel off the paper and allow to cool completely.

4. To make the butter cream: add the sugar to the milk and bring to the boil. Beat the egg yolks, pour on the milk, mix well and return all the mixture to the saucepan. Stir over a gentle heat without boiling until slightly thickened. Strain and leave to cool completely.

5. Beat the butter until creamy and gradually whisk in the custard mixture. Flavour with coffee essence.

6. To make the chocolate caraque: melt the chocolate on a plate over a pan of boiling water. Spread thinly on a marble slab or other hard cold surface. When just set, use a long knife to shave off curls of chocolate: hold the knife with one hand on the handle and one hand on the tip of the blade. Hold it horizontally and scrape the chocolate surface by pulling the knife towards you. Chill the curls to harden them.

7. To decorate: split the cake in half and sandwich with one-third of the butter cream. Spread the tops and sides with the remainder. Press browned chopped almonds on to the sides of the cake. Cover the top with a pile of caraque chocolate and sift over a very fine dusting of icing sugar.

NOTE: If you do not want to make caraque, the cake can be very simply and attractively decorated in the following manner. Melt the chocolate meant for the caraque and stir it into the coffee butter cream. Spread the icing as smoothly as possible on top of the cake. Lightly place a lacy paper doily over it. Sift icing sugar over cake and doily. Carefully remove the doily, taking pains to prevent the icing sugar on it from falling on to the cake.

Génoise Fine

4 eggs
125g/4^1/2 oz caster sugar
100g/3^1/2 oz butter, melted, but cool
100g/3^1/2 oz plain flour

1. Prepare a moule-à-manqué or deep sandwich tin with oil, greaseproof paper, sugar and flour. Set the oven to 190°C/375°F/gas mark 5.

2. Break the eggs into a large bowl and add the sugar. Set the bowl over (not in) a pan of simmering water and whisk until light, fluffy and doubled in bulk. Take off the heat and whisk until cool. Whisk in the butter quickly – if you work slowly the cake will collapse.

3. Sift the flour over the cake mixture and fold it in thoroughly but gently with a large metal spoon.

4. Turn into the prepared tin and bake for 30-35 minutes. Leave to cool in the tin for a few minutes then turn on to a wire rack to cool.

NOTE: This is sometimes called a 'butter sponge'. However, this description is not culinarily correct, as a true sponge contains no fat.

Génoise Commune

4 eggs
125g/4^1/2 oz caster sugar
55g/2oz butter, melted but cool
125g/4^1/2 oz plain flour

1. Set the oven to 190°C/375°F/gas mark 5. Prepare a moule-à-manqué or deep sandwich tin (see page 40).

2. Break the eggs into a bowl. Add the sugar. Place the bowl over a saucepan of simmering water and whisk until the mixture has doubled in bulk, and will leave a ribbon trail on the surface when the whisk is lifted. Lift the bowl off the heat and continue to whisk until the mixture has cooled. (If using an electric beater, whisking need not be done over heat.) Whisk in the butter quickly – if you work too slowly the cake will collapse.

3. Sift the flour over the cake mixture and fold it in thoroughly but gently with a large metal spoon.

4. Pour the mixture into the prepared tin. Bake for 30-35 minutes. Allow to cool slightly before turning out on to a wire rack.

Chocolate Génoise

4 eggs
110g/4oz caster sugar
55g/2oz unsalted butter, melted but cool
85g/3oz plain flour, sifted
30g/1oz cocoa powder, sifted

1. First prepare a 20cm/8 inch moule-à-manqué cake tin. Brush it lightly with oil or melted lard. Line the base with a piece of greaseproof paper cut to size and brush again with oil or lard. Dust first with caster sugar and then with flour. Tip out any excess.

2. Whisk the eggs and sugar together until very light and fluffy. If you have a machine, this should take 5 minutes. If not, the whisking has to be done with a balloon whisk in a bowl set over a saucepan of simmering water and it can take up to 10 minutes. Be careful not to allow the base of the bowl to become too hot.

3. The mixture should then be allowed to cool and should be whisked occasionally for 5 minutes. It is ready when it leaves a ribbon trail when the whisk is lifted. Do not over-whisk and stop if it begins to lose bulk. Whisk in the butter quickly. If you work too slowly the cake will collapse.

4. Fold the flour and cocoa powder into the mixture with a large metal spoon.

5. Tip into the prepared cake tin, give a light tap on the work surface to get rid of any large air pockets and bake in a preheated oven at 190°C/375°F/gas mark 5 for 25-35 minutes.

6. Leave to cool in the tin for 2 minutes and then turn out on to a wire rack to cool completely.

Very Rich Chocolate Cake

This recipe is an adaptation of a Martha Stewart cake.

For the cake:
55g/2oz sultanas, chopped
55ml/2 fl oz brandy
3 eggs, separated
140g/5oz caster sugar
200g/7oz dark chocolate, chopped evenly
30ml/2 tablespoons water
110g/4oz unsalted butter
55g/2oz plain flour
85g/3oz ground almonds

For the icing:
140g/5oz dark chocolate, cut into small pieces
150ml/¼ pint double cream

1. Soak the sultanas in the brandy overnight.

2. Set the oven to 180°C/350°F/gas mark 4.

3. Prepare a moule-à-manqué or 20cm/8 inch cake tin: lightly brush with oil, line the bottom with a circle of greaseproof paper and grease again.

4. Separate the eggs and beat the yolks and sugar until pale and mousse-like.

5. Put the chocolate and water in a bowl set over a saucepan of simmering water. Stir until melted, then stir in the butter piece by piece until the mixture is smooth. Stir into the egg yolk mixture.

6. Sift the flour and very carefully fold it into the egg yolk and chocolate mixture with the ground almonds, sultanas and brandy.

7. Whisk the egg whites until stiff but not dry and fold into the chocolate mixture.

8. Turn the mixture into the prepared tin and bake for 35-40 minutes (the centre should still be moist). Leave to get completely cold in the tin.

9. Remove the cake from the tin and put it on a wire rack to ice it.

10. Prepare the icing: heat together the chocolate and cream. Stir until all the chocolate has melted and the mixture is smooth. Allow to cool and thicken to a coating consistency before pouring it over the cake.

11. Allow the icing to harden for at least 2 hours.

Black Cherry Cake

400g/14oz tin black cherries
Kirsch
290ml/¹/₂ pint double cream
chocolate génoise (see page 55)
85g/3oz dark chocolate, grated
45ml/3 tablespoons water
110g/4oz icing sugar
about 55g/2oz browned split almonds
icing sugar for dusting

1. Remove the stones from the cherries and sprinkle the fruit with a little Kirsch.

2. Whip the cream until it will just hold its shape.

3. Split the cake into 3 thin rounds. On the bottom layer spread about one-third of the cream and sprinkle with half the cherries. Place the next layer of cake on top. Spread on another third of cream and the rest of the cherries. Place the top round on and flatten gently with your hands.

4. Place the chocolate in a pan with the water and stir over gentle heat until smooth, taking care not to boil.

5. Sift the icing sugar into a bowl and blend in the chocolate, adding a little extra water if necessary. Do this drop by drop to make a thick, pouring consistency. Pour over the top of the cake and allow to set.

6. Spread the remaining cream around the sides of the cake and press the browned split almonds against it.

7. Cut 3 strips of paper about 25cm/10 inches long and about 2.5cm/1 inch wide. Place them over the cake about 2.5cm/1 inch apart and sift over a heavy dusting of icing sugar.

8. Remove the paper strips carefully to reveal a striped brown and white top.

Gâteau Nougatine

For the cake:
110g/4oz hazelnuts
4 eggs
1 egg white
117g/4^{1}/$_{4}$ oz sugar
55g/2oz softened butter
100g/3^{1}/$_{2}$ oz plain flour

For the royal icing:
1 small egg white
170g/6oz icing sugar
squeeze of lemon juice

For the nougat:
45g/1^{1}/$_{2}$ oz finely chopped almonds
85g/3oz caster sugar
2.5ml/^{1}/$_{2}$ teaspoon powdered glucose or pinch
    of cream of tartar

For the crème au beurre mousseline:
85g/3oz lump or granulated sugar
45ml/3 tablespoons water
2 egg yolks
110-140g/4-5oz unsalted butter

For the chocolate fondant icing:
225g/8oz loaf sugar
2.5ml/^{1}/$_{2}$ teaspoon liquid glucose or pinch of
    cream of tartar
115ml/4 fl oz water
30g/1oz unsweetened chocolate
1 drop vanilla essence

1. Set the oven to 180°C/350°F/gas mark 4.
Prepare a moule-à-manqué tin with
greaseproof paper, oil, sugar and flour.
Then start with the cake: brown the nuts.
Remove the skins. Cool and grind.

2. Separate the eggs. Beat the yolks and 1
egg white with all but 15ml/1 tablespoon
sugar, until white and creamy. Whisk the
remaining egg whites until stiff. Whisk in
the reserved sugar.

3. Quickly beat the soft butter into the egg-
yolk mixture. Mix the sifted flour with the
nuts, lightly mix into the cake mixture and
finally fold in the meringue mixture.
Then pile into the cake tin. Bake for 40-50
minutes. Cool on a wire rack.

4. For the royal icing: whisk the egg white
until frothy. Beat the icing sugar into it
with the lemon juice until very smooth,
white and stiff. Cover with a damp cloth
until ready for use.

5. Oil a baking sheet. Make the nougat:
bake the chopped almonds until pale
brown. Keep warm. Put the sugar and
glucose into a heavy pan and place over a
moderate heat. When golden, add the
warmed almonds and continue to cook for
1 minute. Then turn on to the oiled baking
sheet. Turn it over with an oiled palette
knife, using a half-mixing, half-kneading
motion. While still warm and pliable, roll
as thinly as possible with an oiled lemon.

6. For the crème au beurre mousseline:
dissolve the sugar in the water. Boil until
the syrup will form short threads when
stretched between finger and thumb.
Whisk the yolks as you pour on the sugar
syrup in a steady stream. Whisk until thick
and mousse-like. Cream the butter and,

when soft, add the mousse to the butter.

7. For the chocolate fondant icing: dissolve the sugar and 2.5ml/^{1}/$_2$ teaspoon liquid glucose in the water over a low heat without boiling. Cover and bring to the boil. Boil to soft ball (110-115°C/230-240°F). Meanwhile, scrub a stainless steel worktop and sprinkle with water. Stop the sugar syrup from cooking further by dipping the bottom of the pan into a bowl of very cold water. Cool slightly.

8. Chop the chocolate and melt it over a pan of simmering water. Pour the sugar syrup slowly on to the moistened stainless steel top. With a wet palette knife, fold the outsides of the mixture into the centre. When opaque but still fairly soft, add the melted chocolate and vanilla essence and continue to turn with a spatula and work until the fondant becomes fairly stiff. Put in a bowl and stand over a saucepan of simmering water to soften.

9. To assemble, split the cake into 3 layers. Crush the nougat with a rolling pin and mix half of it with half the butter cream (crème au beurre mousseline). Sandwich the cake together with this. Pour the melted chocolate fondant icing over the top of the cake. Spread butter cream around the sides and press on the remaining crushed nougat.

10. When the chocolate has set, fill a piping bag fitted with a writing nozzle with the royal icing and pipe the word 'nougatine' across the top of the cake.

All-in-One Chocolate Cake

85g/3oz flour
pinch of salt
30g/1oz cocoa powder
2 eggs
110g/4oz caster sugar
110g/4oz butter
2-3 drops of vanilla essence
30-45ml/2-3 tablespoons warm water
soured cream and chocolate icing (see
  page 152-153)

1. Set the oven to 180°C/350°F/gas mark 4.

2. Sift the flour and salt into a bowl. Add the cocoa powder.

3. Add the eggs, sugar, butter and vanilla essence.

4. Beat with an electric whisk for 2 minutes.

5. Add the warm water and beat for a further minute.

6. Turn into a 10cm/7 inch cake tin and bake for 25-30 minutes. Turn out and leave to cool.

7. Split the cake in half and sandwich it together with half of the icing. Use the remaining icing to cover the top of the cake.

Dobez Torte

This is a cake with 5 layers. The mixture will not deteriorate if all the layers cannot be baked at the same time because of a lack of baking sheets or space in the oven.

SERVES 6
For the cake:
4 eggs
170g/6oz caster sugar
140g/5oz plain flour
pinch of salt

For the butter cream:
85g/3oz granulated sugar
60-75ml/4-5 tablespoons water
3 egg yolks
225g/8oz unsalted butter
coffee essence
55g/2oz skinned, toasted and ground hazelnuts

For the decoration:
140g/5oz sugar
30ml/2 tablespoons browned chopped almonds
  or ground browned hazelnuts
6 whole browned, skinned hazelnuts

1. Set the oven to 190°C/375°F/gas mark 5. Grease and flour 5 baking sheets and mark a 20cm/8 inch circle on each sheet (use a flan ring or saucepan lid in the floured surface).

2. Start with the cake: whisk the eggs, adding the sugar gradually. Set the bowl over (not in) a pan of simmering water and whisk until the mixture is thick and mousse-like. Remove from the heat and whisk intermittently until cool. Sift the

flour and salt and fold into the egg mixture with a metal spoon. Divide the mixture between the 5 baking sheets and spread into circles as marked.

3. Bake for 8 minutes. Trim the edges and leave to cool on a wire rack.

4. Prepare the butter cream: dissolve the sugar in the water and, when clear, boil rapidly to the thread. (To test, put a little sugar syrup on to a wooden spoon, dip your index finger and thumb into cold water and then into the syrup in the spoon. When you pull your finger and thumb apart there should be a thread of syrup between them.) Allow to cool slightly for about 1 minute.

5. Whisk the yolks in a bowl and then pour the syrup slowly on to them, whisking all the time. Keep whisking until you have a thick mousse-like mixture. Cream the butter well and beat in the egg and sugar mixture. Cool. Flavour 30ml/2 tablespoons of the buttercream with coffee essence and keep for decoration. Mix the ground hazelnuts and the remaining coffee essence into the remaining mixture.

6. Lay one piece of cake on a wire rack over an oiled tray. Melt the sugar for the caramel in a little water and, when dissolved, boil fiercely until a good caramel colour and pour immediately over the piece of cake, covering it completely.

7. Allow to harden slightly and mark into 6

portions with an oiled knife. (The idea is to cut through the setting caramel but not through the cake.) Trim the edges of excess caramel.

8. Sandwich the cake layers together with the coffee and hazelnut butter cream, placing the one with caramel on top. Spread the coffee and hazelnut butter cream thinly around the sides and press on the nuts.

9. Using a forcing bag with a large fluted nozzle, pipe a rosette with the remaining plain butter cream on top of each portion of cake. Decorate each rosette with a whole browned hazelnut.

Black Sticky Gingerbread

225g/8oz butter
225g/8oz soft brown sugar
225g/8oz black treacle
340g/12oz plain flour
10ml/2 teaspoons ground ginger
15ml/1 tablespoon ground cinnamon
10ml/2 teaspoons bicarbonate of soda
2 beaten eggs
290ml/^{1}/$_2$ pint milk

1. Grease a 20 x 30cm/8 x 12 inches roasting pan and line the base with greaseproof paper.

2. Preheat the oven to 150°C/300°F/gas mark 2.

3. Melt the butter, soft brown sugar and treacle in a pan.

4. Sift the flour, ground ginger and cinnamon, then stir in the melted mixture with the beaten eggs. Warm the milk to blood heat, pour it on to the bicarbonate of soda, stir it in and add it to the mixture. Stir well and pour the mixture into the prepared tin.

5. Bake the gingerbread for about 1^1/$_2$ hours . Cover the top with greaseproof paper after 1 hour.

6. When the gingerbread is cold, cut it into fingers and serve it spread with butter. This gingerbread keeps very well: in fact, it improves.

Kulich

This Russian Easter cake recipe has been adapted from a recipe in the *Observer Guide to European Cookery* by Jane Grigson.

570g/1¼ lb flour, sifted
1 packet dried yeast
180ml/6 fl oz warm milk
1.25ml/¼ teaspoon salt
3 egg yolks
140g/5oz sugar
3 cardamom pods, seeded and crushed
140g/5oz butter, softened
3 egg whites, stiffly whisked
75g/2½ oz raisins
30g/1oz each candied fruit and blanched
   almonds, chopped

For decoration (optional):
blanched almonds, chopped, candied fruit and
   peel or white glacé icing

1. Mix 225g/8oz of the flour with the yeast in a mixing bowl, then stir in the milk. Put the mixture into a polythene bag, put in a warm place and leave till spongy and doubled in size – about 1 hour.

2. Mix in the salt, 2½ egg yolks (set aside about half a yolk for glazing the kulich afterwards), sugar, cardamom and butter. Then fold in the egg whites and 225g/8oz more flour. The dough will be on the wet and sticky side. Add the rest of the flour gradually until the dough leaves the sides of the bowl. If it is a little sticky, do not worry too much. Put in a warm place and leave to rise again – about 2-3 hours this time.

3. Knock down the dough and add the fruits and almonds. Divide between 2 buttered and floured tall round moulds. If you have no suitable moulds (such as large brioche tins) use coffee tins. The dough should come half or two-thirds of the way up the tins. Leave to prove for about 1 hour.

4. Preheat the oven to 180°C/350°F/gas mark 4. Bake the kulichs in the oven for about 45 minutes. Check after 35 minutes by inserting a cocktail stick or thin skewer, which should come out clean. When the dough is cooked, the cake should have the appearance of a chef's hat.

5. When ready, turn out and brush with the remaining egg yolk and decorate, if you like, with chopped fruit and nuts, or icing, pouring it on so that it dribbles down the sides. Stick a candle in the top of each cake (if it is Easter).

Scones

MAKES 6
225g/8oz plain flour
15ml/1 tablespoon baking powder
2.5ml/1/2 teaspoon salt
55g/2oz butter
30g/1oz sugar (optional)
150ml/1/4 pint milk

For glazing:
1 egg, beaten

1. Set the oven to 220°C/425°F/gas mark 7. Flour a baking sheet. Sift the flour with the other powder ingredients. Then rub in the butter until the mixture resembles breadcrumbs. Stir in the sugar if required.

2. Make a deep well in the flour, pour in all the liquid and mix to a soft, spongy dough with a palette knife.

3. On a floured surface, knead the dough very lightly until it is just smooth. Roll or press out to about 2.5cm/1 inch thick and stamp into small rounds. Brush the scones with beaten egg for a glossy crust or sprinkle with flour for a soft one.

4. Bake the scones at the top of the hot oven for 7 minutes or until well risen and brown. Leave to cool on a wire rack, or serve hot from the oven.

NOTE: 30g/1oz sultanas or other dried fruit may be added to the dried ingredients. For cheese scones, substitute 30g/1oz grated strong cheese for half the butter, and omit the sugar.

Coffee Buns

MAKES 12
110g/4oz butter
110g/4oz caster sugar
2 eggs
110g/4oz self-raising flour
10ml/2 teaspoons instant coffee powder
1.25ml/1/4 teaspoon vanilla essence
55g/2oz chopped walnuts
55g/2oz chocolate

1. Set the oven to 180°C/350°F/gas mark 4. Grease and flour 12 bun tins or paper moulds.

2. Cream the butter and sugar until light and fluffy.

3. Beat in the eggs, a little at a time.

4. Fold in the flour, coffee, vanilla essence and chopped nuts. Add a little water if necessary to make a soft dropping consistency.

5. Fill the tins or paper moulds two-thirds full and bake for 15-20 minutes. Leave to cool on a wire rack.

6. Grate the chocolate. Melt it on a plate over a pan of boiling water

7. Spread each bun with a little melted chocolate and leave to cool and harden.

Shortbread

MAKES 6-8
110g/4oz butter
55g/2oz caster sugar
110g/4oz plain flour
55g/2oz rice flour

1. Set the oven to 170°C/325°F/gas mark 3.

2. Beat the butter until soft, add the sugar and beat until pale and creamy.

3. Sift in the flours and work to a smooth paste.

4. Place a 15cm/6 inch flan ring on a baking sheet and press the shortbread paste into a neat circle. Remove the flan ring and flatten the paste slightly with a rolling pin. Crimp the edges. Prick lightly.

5. Mark the shortbread into 6 or 8 wedges, sprinkle lightly with a little extra caster sugar and bake for 40 minutes until a pale biscuit colour. Leave to cool for 2 minutes and then lift on to a cooling rack to cool completely.

Flavoured Shortbreads

Shortbread can be stamped into biscuits or made into petticoat tails and put into attractive tins. There are many variations that can be made by adding different ingredients to the basic recipe (see left).

ALMOND SHORTBREAD
Add 85g/3oz ground almonds with the flour to the creamed butter and sugar.

HAZELNUT SHORTBREAD
Add 110g/4oz roughly chopped, browned and skinned hazelnuts with the flour to the creamed butter and sugar.

GINGER SHORTBREAD
Add 5ml/1 teaspoon of ground ginger and 55g/2oz chopped crystallized stem ginger with the flour.

ORANGE SHORTBREAD
Add the finely grated rind of 2 oranges to the creamed butter and sugar before adding the flour.

Iced Biscuits

MAKES 20
110g/4oz unsalted butter
110g/4oz caster sugar
1 egg, beaten
a few drops vanilla flavouring
285g/10oz plain flour
pinch of salt

For the glacé icing:
225g/8oz icing sugar
boiling water
colouring (optional)

1. Set the oven to 190°C/375°F/gas mark 5.

2. Beat the butter and, when soft, add the sugar and beat again until light and fluffy. Gradually beat in the egg. Add the vanilla flavouring.

3. Sift the flour with the salt and mix it into the butter, sugar and egg. Then roll the paste out thinly (about the thickness of a heavy coin) and stamp into rounds with a cutter. Place on an ungreased baking sheet.

4. Bake for 8-10 minutes until just beginning to brown at the edges. Leave to cool on a wire rack.

5. Make the glacé icing: sift the icing sugar into a bowl. Add enough boiling water to mix to a fairly stiff consistency.

6. Colour the icing as required. Then spoon the icing smoothly and evenly over the top of the biscuits. Leave to dry and harden.

Peanut Butter Cookies

MAKES ABOUT 40 BISCUITS
140g/5oz butter
110g/4oz caster sugar
110g/4oz soft brown sugar
1 large egg, beaten
110g/4oz crunchy peanut butter
2.5ml/1/2 teaspoon vanilla essence
200g/7oz plain flour
2.5ml/1/2 teaspoon salt
5ml/1 teaspoon baking powder

1. Heat the oven to 180°C/350°F/gas mark 4.

2. Cream the butter and both sugars together until smooth and soft. Beat in the egg, then the peanut butter, and add the vanilla.

3. Sift the flour with the salt and the baking powder into the mixture and stir until smooth. Do not over-beat or the dough will be oily.

4. Roll the mixture into small balls with the fingers and place well apart on 3 ungreased baking sheets. Flatten with the prongs of a fork.

5. Bake for 10-15 minutes, to an even, not too dark, brown.

6. While hot, ease off the baking sheets with a palette knife or fish slice and cool on a wire rack. Once stone cold and crisp, store in an airtight container.

Flapjacks

MAKES 16
170g/6oz butter
110g/4oz demerara sugar
55g/2oz golden syrup
225g/8oz rolled oats

1. Set the oven to 190°C/375°F/gas mark 5.

2. Melt the butter in a saucepan.

3. Weigh out the sugar, then weigh the syrup by spooning it on top of the sugar (thus preventing it sticking to the scale pan) and add to the melted butter to heat through.

4. Remove the pan from the heat and stir in the oats.

5. Spread the mixture into a well-greased shallow tin.

6. Bake in the oven for about 30 minutes until golden brown.

7. Remove from the oven, mark immediately into bars and leave in the tin to cool.

Easter Biscuits

MAKES 8
55g/2oz butter
55g/2oz caster sugar
grated rind of 1/2 lemon
1/2 egg or 1 yolk
110g/4oz plain flour
2.5ml/1/2 teaspoon caraway seeds
55g/2oz currants
30g/1oz granulated sugar

1. Set the oven to 180°C/350°F/gas mark 4. Cover a baking sheet with a piece of greaseproof paper.

2. Cream together the butter, caster sugar and lemon rind. Beat in the egg.

3. Fold in the flour, caraway and currants.

4. Roll out the dough on a floured board to 5mm/1/4 inch thick. Cut into large rounds and carefully lift them on to the baking sheet. Prick with a fork and sprinkle with granulated sugar.

5. Bake for 10-15 minutes until set and pale golden.

6. Remove from the oven and leave on a wire rack to crisp and cool.

NOTE: If the dough becomes soft and difficult to handle, wrap it up and chill for 15 minutes before proceeding.

CAKES, SCONES, BUNS AND BISCUITS 67

Old-Fashioned Gingerbread

MAKES ABOUT 120 SMALL BISCUITS
340g/12oz plain flour
5ml/1 teaspoon baking powder
5ml/1 teaspoon salt
5ml/1 teaspoon grated nutmeg
5ml/1 teaspoon ground cloves
10ml/2 teaspoons ground cinnamon
10ml/2 teaspoons ground ginger
225g/8oz butter
225g/8oz caster sugar
170g/6oz dark brown sugar
2 eggs, beaten

1. Set the oven to 180°C/350°F/gas mark 4. Then sift the flour, baking powder, salt and spices into a large bowl.

2. Melt the butter in a saucepan, add the caster sugar and dark brown sugar, mix well and allow to cool. Add the beaten eggs. Make a well in the dry ingredients and gradually add the butter and sugar mixture. Place in the refrigerator until completely cold.

3. Cut into 4 pieces and roll each one out separately until the thickness of a pound coin. Stamp into different shapes, e.g. stars, balls, angels, Christmas trees. Place on a greased baking sheet and bake in batches in the preheated oven for about 10 minutes.

NOTE: This mixture should be made by hand. It is very easy to overwork.

Almond and Apricot Cookies

MAKES 18
85g/3oz butter
85g/3oz granulated sugar
110g/4oz ground almonds

For the decoration:
apricot jam
flaked almonds, browned

1. Set the oven to 180°C/350°F/gas mark 4.

2. Cream the butter and, when soft, add the sugar and beat until light and fluffy. Stir in the ground almonds and roll the paste into balls the size of a marble. Chill for 10 minutes.

3. Place each ball in a paper case and put the cases into patty moulds. Bake in the oven for 15-20 minutes. Allow to cool in their cases.

4. Remove from the cases, spread with a little apricot jam and decorate with a browned flaked almond.

Brandy Snap Cups

MAKES 8
110g/4oz sugar
110g/4oz butter
110g/4oz or 60ml/4 tablespoons golden syrup
110g/4oz flour
juice of 1 lemon
large pinch of ground ginger

To serve:
whipped cream or ice cream

1. Set the oven to 190°C/375°F/gas mark 5. Grease a baking sheet, palette knife and one end of a wide rolling pin or a narrow jam jar or bottle.

2. Melt the sugar, butter and syrup together. Remove from the heat.

3. Sift in the flour, stirring well. Add the lemon juice and ginger.

4. Put the mixture on the baking sheet in teaspoonfuls about 15cm/6 inches apart. Bake for 5-7 minutes. They should go golden brown but still be soft.
Watch carefully as they burn easily. Remove from the oven.

5. When cool enough to handle, lever each biscuit off the baking sheet with a greased palette knife.

6. Working quickly, shape them around the end of the rolling pin or greased jam jar to form a cup-shaped mould.

7. When the biscuits have taken shape, remove them and leave to cool on a wire rack.

8. Serve filled with whipped cream or ice cream.

NOTE I: If the brandy snaps are not to be served immediately they must, once cool, be put into an airtight container for storage. They become soggy if left out. Similarly, brandy snaps should not be filled with moist mixtures like whipped cream or ice cream until shortly before serving, or they will quickly lose their crispness.

NOTE II: Do not bake too many snaps at one time as once they are cold, they are too brittle to shape. They can be made pliable again if returned to the oven.

Brandy Snaps

The mixture for these is exactly the same as for brandy snap cups (page 68) but the biscuits are shaped round a thick wooden spoon handle and not over the end of a rolling pin or jam jar. They are filled with whipped cream from a piping bag fitted with a medium nozzle.

Miniature brandy snaps (served as petits fours after dinner) are shaped over a skewer. There are not generally filled.

Gingernuts

MAKES 20-25
30g/1oz demerara sugar
55g/2oz butter
85g/3oz golden syrup
110g/4oz flour
2.5ml/$\frac{1}{2}$ teaspoon bicarbonate of soda
7ml/1 heaped teaspoon ground ginger

1. Set the oven to 180°C/350°F/gas mark 4. Grease a baking sheet.

2. Melt the brown sugar, butter and syrup together slowly, without boiling. Make sure the sugar has dissolved. Allow to cool.

3. Sift the flour, bicarbonate of soda and ground ginger into a mixing bowl. Make a well in the centre.

4. Pour the melted mixture into the well and knead until smooth. Roll into balls and flatten, on the prepared baking sheet, into biscuits about 3.5cm/1$\frac{1}{2}$ inches diameter.

5. Bake for 20-25 minutes or until golden brown. The gingernuts will not be crisp until they cool and set.

Mince Pies

MAKES 20–24 TARTS
*340g/12oz flour quantity well-chilled rich
  shortcrust pastry (see page 86)*
450g/1lb mincemeat (see page 112)

For the glaze:
beaten egg or milk

To serve:
icing sugar

1. Set the oven to 190°C/375°F/gas mark 5.

2. Divide the pastry in half and roll one half out thinly and use it to line tartlet tins. Then fill each tartlet tin with enough mincemeat to come about three-quarters of the way up the pastry.

3. Roll out the remaining pastry and either stamp into shapes, such as stars, dampen lightly with water and press firmly but gently on top of the mincemeat *or* cut into circles to fit the tarts as lids. Dampen the pastry edges and press the tops down lightly, sealing the edges carefully.

4. Brush your chosen glaze on the lids – the milk will give a matt finish, and the beaten egg a shiny finish.

5. Snip the lids with a pair of scissors or sharp knife to make a small slit for the steam to escape, leaving the shapes untouched.

6. Bake for 20 minutes until light golden brown.

7. Cool on a wire rack.

8. Serve warm sprinkled with icing sugar.

NOTE: Once completely cold, mince pies can be frozen or stored in an airtight container.

FORTIFIED SWEET WHITE

Langues de Chat

MAKES 30-40
100g/3¹/2 oz butter
100g/3¹/2 oz caster sugar
3 egg whites
100g/3¹/2 oz plain flour

1. Set the oven to 200°C/400°F/gas mark 6. Grease a baking sheet or line with silicone paper.

2. Soften the butter with a wooden spoon and add the sugar gradually. Beat until pale and fluffy.

3. Whisk the egg whites slightly and add gradually to the mixture, beating thoroughly between each addition.

4. Sift the flour and fold into the mixture with a metal spoon. Put into a forcing bag fitted with a medium-sized plain nozzle. Pipe into fingers the thickness of a pencil and about 5cm/2 inches long.

5. Tap the baking sheet on the table to release any over-large air bubbles from the fingers. Bake for 5-7 minutes or until biscuit-coloured in the middle and brown at the edges. Cool slightly, then lift off the baking sheet with a palette knife.
Cool completely before putting into an airtight container.

Macaroons

MAKES 25
110g/4oz ground almonds
170g/6oz caster sugar
5ml/1 teaspoon plain flour
2 egg whites
2 drops vanilla essence
rice paper for baking
split almonds for decoration

1. Set the oven to 180°C/350°F/gas mark 4.

2. Mix the almonds, sugar and flour together.

3. Add the egg whites and vanilla. Beat very well.

4. Lay a sheet of rice paper or vegetable parchment on a baking sheet and with a teaspoon put on small heaps of the mixture, well apart.

5. Place a split almond on each macaroon and bake for 20 minutes. Allow to cool.

NOTE I: To use this recipe for petits fours the mixture must be put out in very tiny blobs on the rice paper. Two macaroons can then be sandwiched together with a little stiff apricot jam and served in petits fours paper cases.

NOTE II: Ratafia biscuits are tiny macaroons with added almond essence.

Sponge Fingers

MAKES 30
6 eggs
140g/5oz caster sugar
110g/4oz flour
30g/1oz arrowroot

1. Set the oven to 200°C/400°F/gas mark 6. Line 2 large baking sheets with silicone baking paper. Draw parallel lines 12.5cm/5 inches apart on the paper.

2. Separate 5 of the eggs. Beat the yolks with the whole egg and 110g/4oz of the caster sugar in a large bowl until they are nearly white.

3. Whisk the egg whites until stiff and gradually whisk in the remaining caster sugar. Fold the egg whites into the egg-yolk and sugar mixture. Carefully fold in the sifted flour and arrowroot.

4. Fit a 5mm/¼ inch plain nozzle into a piping bag and fill the bag with the mixture. Pipe 12.5cm/5 inch fingers between the parallel lines on the baking paper. The fingers should be just touching.

5. Place in the top of the oven for about 10 minutes or until the sponge has risen and is biscuit-coloured.

6. Remove them from the oven, invert on to a clean tea towel and immediately and carefully peel off the paper. Turn the sponge fingers on to a wire rack to cool.

Tuiles à l'Orange

MAKES 25
2 egg whites
110g/4oz caster sugar
55g/2oz butter
55g/2oz plain flour
grated rind of 1 orange

1. Set the oven to 190°C/375°F/gas mark 5. Grease a baking sheet, or line with silicone paper.

2. Whisk the egg whites until stiff. Add the sugar and whisk thoroughly.

3. Melt the butter. Add it to the meringue mixture by degrees with the sifted flour. Fold in the orange rind.

4. Spread out teaspoonfuls very thinly on the prepared baking sheet, keeping them well apart to allow for spreading during cooking. Bake until golden brown (5-6 minutes).

5. Oil a rolling pin or the handle of a large wooden spoon. Loosen the tuiles from the baking sheet while still hot. While they are still warm and pliable curl them over the rolling pin or round the wooden spoon handle. When they are quite firm slip them off. When cold, store in an airtight container.

NOTE: Using silicone paper guarantees that the tuiles will not stick.

Tuiles Amandines

MAKES 25

30g/1oz blanched almonds
2 egg whites
110g/4oz caster sugar
55g/2oz plain flour
2.5ml/1/2 teaspoon vanilla essence
55g/2oz melted butter

1. Set the oven to 180°C/350°F, gas mark 4. Lightly grease at least 3 baking sheets and a rolling pin or line baking sheets with silicone paper.

2. Cut the almonds into fine slivers or shreds.

3. Place the egg whites in a bowl. Beat in the sugar with a fork. The egg white should be frothy but by no means snowy. Sift in the flour and add the vanilla and almonds. Mix with the fork.

4. Cool the butter (it should be melted but not hot) and add it to the mixture. Stir well.

5. Place the mixture in teaspoonfuls at least 13cm/5 inches apart on the baking sheets and flatten well.

6. Bake in the oven until a good brown at the edges and pale biscuit-coloured in the middle (about 6 minutes). Remove from the oven and cool for a few seconds.

7. Lift the biscuits off carefully with a palette knife. Lay them, while still warm and pliable, over the rolling pin to form them into a slightly curved shape. As soon as they are stone cold put them into an airtight tin or plastic bag to keep them crisp.

NOTE: Using silicone paper guarantees that the tuiles will not stick.

Venetian Biscuits

MAKES 24
110g/4oz blanched almonds
450g/1lb flour
pinch of salt
5ml/1 teaspoon baking powder
140g/5oz granulated sugar
85g/3oz plain chocolate, chopped into small
  pieces
4 large eggs, lightly beaten
1 egg white, to glaze

1. Preheat the oven to 190°C/375°F/gas mark 5. Grease a baking sheet.

2. Place the almonds on the baking sheet and bake in the oven until golden brown. Cool. Chop two-thirds and grind the remaining third finely.

3. Sift the flour, salt and baking powder into a bowl. Add the sugar, chocolate and almonds. Mix well.

4. Make a well in the centre and add the beaten eggs. Gradually incorporate the dry ingredients with the eggs. The dough should be firm.

5. Divide the dough into 4 and roll each piece into a long thin sausage shape approximately 2cm/³/₄ inch in diameter and 20cm/8 inches long.

6. Place the rolls on the baking sheet at least 5cm/2 inches apart. Lightly whisk the egg white until just frothy and brush over the tops of the rolls.

7. Place in the preheated oven and bake for 20 minutes.

8. Remove the rolls from the oven, reduce the heat to 105°C/225°F/gas mark ¹/₄. Cut the rolls at a 45-degree angle at 1cm/¹/₂ inch intervals and return them individually to the baking sheet. Put back in the oven for a further 30 minutes. Allow to cool completely before serving.

NOTE: Raisins or glacé fruit can be used in place of the chocolate. The biscuits are meant to be eaten after being dipped in a liqueur, e.g. Amaretto or Grappa.

Florentine Biscuits

MAKES 20
55g/2oz butter
55g/2oz sugar
10ml/2 teaspoons honey
55g/2oz plain flour
45g/1¹/₂oz chopped candied peel
45g/1¹/₂oz chopped glacé cherries
45g/1¹/₂oz chopped blanched almonds
85g/3oz chocolate, melted

1. Set the oven to 180°C/350°F/gas mark 4. Grease and flour 2 baking sheets.

2. Melt the butter, sugar and honey together in a heavy pan. Draw off the heat and add the flour, peel, cherries and almonds. Mix until smooth.

3. Drop teaspoonfuls of the mixture on to the baking sheets, leaving plenty of space for them to spread during cooking. Spread slightly with the spoon.

4. Bake for 8-10 minutes until golden. Leave on the tray for 2 minutes and then place on a wire rack to cool.

5. When cold spread the flat sides with melted chocolate. When the chocolate is on the point of setting, mark it with wavy lines with the prongs of a fork. Leave until the chocolate cools and hardens.

Almond Squares

1. Follow the instructions on page 98-99.

2. Set the oven to 200°C/400°F/gas mark 6.

3. Roll the pastry on a floured baking sheet into a rectangle 25 x 20cm/10 x 8inches. Cut into 5cm/2 inch squares.

4. Put a spoonful of the filling into the centre of each piece of pastry. Fold each corner into the middle and press it down lightly into the almond paste to stick it in position.

5. Prove for 15 minutes (put into a warm, draught-free place to allow the dough to rise). Press down the middle of the squares.

6. Brush with beaten egg and bake for 15-20 minutes.

7. When cool, spoon over the freshly made glacé icing.

Orange Tartlets

MAKES 24
rich shortcrust pastry made with 170g/6oz
  flour (see page 86)

For the candied orange zest:
1 medium orange
340g/12oz granulated sugar
45ml/3 tablespoons liquid glucose
90ml/6 tablespoons water

For the orange curd:
1 large orange
1 medium lemon
55g/2oz unsalted butter
110g/4oz caster sugar
4 egg yolks

1. To make the candied orange zest:
remove the zest from the orange with a
potato peeler or small sharp knife and cut
into 5mm/¼ inch strips. Put into a small
saucepan with enough water to cover and
boil for 5 minutes to remove the bitter
taste. Drain and refresh under running
cold water.

2. Bring 225g/8oz of the sugar, the liquid
glucose and water up to the boil in the
saucepan. Remove from the heat and stir
in the zest. Allow to stand for 30 minutes.
Bring the liquid back to the boil and allow
to stand for another 30 minutes. Remove
the zest with a fork and transfer to a wire
rack to cool. Put the remaining sugar on a
plate and roll the orange strips in sugar.
Once they are dry they can be stored in an
airtight container at room temperature for
up to a week.

3. Preheat the oven to 180°C/350°F/gas
mark 4. Line small tartlet tins or petit four
tins with the pastry. Prick with a fork and
place in the refrigerator to relax.

4. Bake the tartlet cases blind for 10
minutes (see below). Remove the paper
and beans and bake until the pastry is dry
and light brown. Cool.

5. Next make the curd: grate the rind of the
orange and half the lemon on the finest
gauge of the grater, taking care to grate
only the rind, not the pith. Squeeze the
juice from the orange and lemon.

6. Put the rind, juice, butter, sugar and
lightly beaten egg yolks into a heavy
saucepan or double boiler and heat gently,
stirring all the time, until the mixture is
thick. Strain into a bowl and allow to cool.

7. To assemble: using a piping bag and
very small plain nozzle, pipe a round of
curd into each shell. Cut the orange peel
into small diamonds and use them to
garnish the tartlets.

NOTE: To bake blind, line the raw pastry
case with a piece of foil or a double sheet
of greaseproof paper and fill it with dried
lentils, beans, rice or even pebbles or coins.
This is to prevent the pastry bubbling up
during cooking. When the pastry is half
cooked (about 15 minutes) the 'blind
beans' can be removed and the empty
pastry case further dried out in the oven.
The beans can be re-used indefinitely.

Crosses

1. Follow the instructions on page 98-99.

2. Set the oven to 200°C/400°F/gas mark 6.

3. Roll the pastry out thinly on a floured baking sheet and cut it into 13cm/5 inch squares.

4. Cut through each square and then overlap the 2 opposite corners.

5. Fill the central hole with almond paste filling or apple purée.

6. Prove for 15 minutes in a warm, draught-free place.

7. Brush with beaten egg and bake for 15-20 minutes.

8. When cool, dust with icing sugar or spoon over freshly made glacé icing.

Pinwheels

1. Follow the instructions on page 98-99.

2. Set the oven to 200°C/400°F/gas mark 6.

3. Roll the pastry out thinly on a floured baking sheet and cut it into 13cm/5 inch squares. From each corner, towards the centre of each square, make a cut about 3cm/1½ inches long. Put a blob of almond filling in the uncut centre of each square.

4. Fold alternate points of pastry (one from each corner) into the middle and press on to the filling to secure. This leaves one unfolded point at each corner, and the pastry should now resemble a child's pinwheel.

5. Prove in a warm place for 15 minutes (allow to rise and puff up). Press down the corners.

6. Brush with beaten egg and bake for 15-20 minutes.

7. When cool, spoon on the freshly made glacé icing.

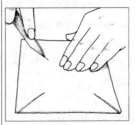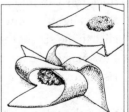

Cut and fill as in recipe

Cinnamon Wheels

In this recipe the almond paste is replaced with a cinnamon filling.

For the cinnamon filling:
55g/2oz butter
55g/2oz sugar
10ml/2 teaspoons cinnamon
small handful of dried fruit and chopped
*   mixed peel*

1. Follow the instructions on page 76, omitting the almond filling.

2. To make the filling, cream the butter with the sugar. Add the cinnamon and mix well.

3. Set the oven to 200°C/400°F/gas mark 6. Roll the pastry to a rectangle 25 x 20cm/10 x 8 inches. Place on a floured baking sheet.

4. Spread the butter mixture over the dough, leaving a narrow margin all around. Scatter over the dried fruit and chopped peel.

5. Roll the pastry, from one end, into a thick roll. Cut into 2.5cm/1 inch slices. With a lightly floured hand, flatten each slice to the size of the palm of your hand. Put somewhere warm and draught-free to rise (prove) for 15 minutes.

6. Brush with egg glaze and bake for 15 minutes.

7. Allow to cool slightly and spoon over the freshly made glacé icing.

Crescents

1. Follow the instructions on page 98-99.

2. Set the oven to 200°C/400°F/gas mark 6. Roll out the pastry, on a floured baking sheet, into a rectangle 30 x 15cm/12 x 6 inches. Cut into 7.5cm/3 inch squares and cut each square diagonally in half.

3. Place a small piece of almond paste at the base (long side) of each triangle. Roll it up from the base to the tip and curve into a crescent shape.

4. Put into a warm, draught-free place to rise (prove) for 15 minutes.

5. Bake for 15-20 minutes or until a good brown. When cool, spoon over the freshly made glacé icing.

Palmiers

Palmiers are usually made from leftover pieces of puff pastry.

1. Set the oven to 200°C/400°F/gas mark 6.

2. Do not roll the trimmings up into a ball as you would with shortcrust pastry – this would spoil the carefully created layers in the paste. Lay the strips or pieces flat on top of each other, folding them if necessary.

3. Using caster sugar instead of flour, roll the pastry out into an oblong 5mm/1/4 inch thick. Sprinkle well with caster sugar. Fold each end of the pastry to the centre, and then fold the pastry in half. Cut the roll across into slices 1cm/1/2 inch wide.

4. Lay the slices flat on a wet baking sheet, far apart, and flatten well with a sugared rolling pin or your hand. Bake for 10 minutes or until pale brown, with the underside caramelized. Turn over and bake for a further 10 minutes. Cool on a wire rack.

NOTE: These are delicious if sandwiched together with strawberry jam and whipped cream.

Tommies

MAKES ABOUT 20
70g/2¹/₂oz caster sugar
110g/4oz butter
85g/3oz ground hazelnuts
140g/5oz plain flour
honey
225g/8oz dark chocolate

1. Set the oven to 180°C/350°F/gas mark 4.

2. Cream the sugar and butter together until white. Stir in the hazelnuts and flour.

3. As soon as the mixture becomes a paste, wrap and leave it in the refrigerator for 30 minutes.

4. Roll out thinly and cut into 2.5cm/1 inch rounds with a biscuit cutter or an upturned glass. Place on a baking sheet and bake for 12 minutes. Put on a wire rack to cool.

5. Spread honey on half the biscuits, then sandwich them with the others. Return to the cooling rack.

6. Warm the chocolate on a plate over a pan of hot water until it has melted and there are no lumps.

7. Spoon over the chocolate to cover the biscuits completely.

8. When set (and if there is enough chocolate left), fill a small piping bag fitted with a writing nozzle with melted chocolate and pipe a design over the set chocolate. Store in an airtight container.

Pastry
and
Batters

Pastry and Batters

PASTRY comes in many forms. All of them are made from a mixture of flour and liquid, and usually contain fat. Variations in quantities and the ingredients themselves give each type its distinctive texture and taste.

The three commonest types of pastry are short (or crumbly), flaky, and choux pastry, all of which have variations. The degree of shortness (or crisp crumbliness) depends on the amount and type of fat (the shortening factor) incorporated into the flour, and the way in which the uncooked pastry, or 'paste', is handled.

THE INGREDIENTS

FATS. Butter gives a crisp, rich shortcrust pastry with excellent flavour. Solid margarine gives a similar result that is slightly less rich and flavourful. Lard gives very short but rather tasteless pastry. It gives excellent results when used with butter. Solid cooking fat and vegetable shortening give a crust similar to lard. Suet is used only in suet crust, which is a soft and rather heavy pastry. A raising agent is usually added to the flour to combat the pastry's doughiness, and to make it more cake-like in texture.

FLOUR in shortcrust pastry is usually plain, all-purpose flour. Weak or cake flour is also suitable for pastry making. Wholemeal flour produces a delicious nutty-flavoured crust, but is more absorbent than white flour and will need more liquid, which makes it harder and heavier. For this reason, a mixture of wholewheat and white flour, usually half and half, is generally used to make 'wholemeal' pastry. Self-raising flour is occasionally used in pastry-making. It produces a soft, thicker, more cakey crust. It is also sometimes used to lighten cheese dough and other heavy pastes like suet crust. Whatever the flour, it should be sifted, even if it has no lumps in it, to incorporate air and give the pastry lightness.

LIQUID. The less liquid used in pastry-making the better. Some very rich doughs, such as almond pastry, which contains a high proportion of butter and eggs, can be kneaded without any water or milk at all. Others need a little liquid to bind them. Water gives the pastry crispness and firmness. Too much makes pastry easy to handle but gives a concrete-hard crust that shrinks in the oven. The addition of egg or egg white instead of water will give a firm but not hard crust. Egg yolk on its own produces a rich, soft and crumbly crust.

MAKING PASTRY

RUBBING IN. Shortcrust pastry is made by rubbing fat into sifted flour and other dry ingredients with the fingertips, then adding other ingredients such as egg yolks and any liquid. Everything should be kept as cool as possible. If the fat melts, the finished pastry may be tough. Cut the fat, which should be firm and cold but not hard, into tiny pieces using a small knife and floured fingers. The flour prevents the fat from sticking to the fingers and beginning to melt, and the smaller the pieces of fat, the better the chances of even distribution. Mix the pieces of fat into the flour, then rub in, handling the fat as quickly and lightly as possible so it does not stick to the fingertips. Pick up a few pieces of floury fat and plenty of flour with the fingertips and thumbs of both hands. Hold your hands about 25cm/10 inches above the bowl, thumbs up and little fingers down, and gently and quickly rub the little pieces of fat into the flour, squashing the fat lightly as you go. Do not try to mash each piece of fat; a breadcrumb texture, not doughy lumps, is what is wanted. Drop the floury flakes of fat from a height; this cools the fat and aerates it, making the finished pastry lighter. Shake the bowl regularly so that the big unrubbed pieces of fat come to the surface. When the mixture looks like very coarse – not fine – breadcrumbs, stop.

ADDING LIQUID. Rich shortcrust pastry, with a higher proportion of fat, needs little, if any, water added. Although over-moist pastry is easy to handle and roll out, the baked crust will be tough and may well shrink in the oven as the water evaporates in the heat. The drier and more difficult to handle the pastry is, the crisper the shortcrust will be. Add only as much water as is needed to get the pastry to hold together, and sprinkle it, 5ml/1 teaspoonful at a time, over as large a surface as possible.

MIXING should be kept to a minimum. Mix the pastry with a fork or knife so you handle it as little as possible. As soon as it holds together in lumps, stop mixing. Lightly flour your hands and quickly and gently gather into a ball, rolling it around the bowl to pick up crumbs.

RELAXING. It is important to chill pastry for at least 30 minutes before rolling it out, or at least before baking. This allows cells to swell and absorb the liquid evenly. 'Relaxed' pastry will not shrink drastically or unevenly as just-made pastry will. Most pastries benefit from chilling, especially in hot weather, or if they are used to line tart tins, when shrinkage can spell disaster. Relaxing is less important, though still a good idea, for pastes used to cover pies. To prevent the surface of the pastry from drying out and cracking in the dry atmosphere of the refrigerator, cover it lightly with cling film or a damp cloth. Ideally pastry is relaxed before and after rolling.

ROLLING OUT. Lightly dust the work surface with flour. Do not use much as this can alter the proportion of flour to the other ingredients. Once rolled, allow the pastry to relax in a cool place before baking, especially if it was not relaxed before rolling out.

TYPES OF PASTRY

SHORTCRUST. See recipe on page 86.

RICH SHORTCRUST. See recipe on page 86.

SUET CRUST PASTRY. This is made like shortcrust pastry except that the fat (suet) is generally chopped or shredded before use. Because self-raising flour (or plain flour and baking powder) is used in order to produce a less heavy dough pastry, it is important to cook the pastry soon after making it, while the raising agent is at its most active. During cooking the raising agent causes the dough to puff up and rise slightly and as it hardens, air will be trapped. This makes the suet crust lighter and more bread- like (see page 88).

PÂTE SUCRÉE, ALMOND PASTRY AND PATE A PATÉ. These and other very rich pastries are extreme forms of rich shortcrust, with all the liquid replaced by fat or eggs. Traditionally they are made by working together the egg yolks and fat, and sometimes sugar, with the fingertips until soft and creamy (see page 95-6). The flour is then gradually incorporated until a soft, very rich paste is achieved. To mix the paste, use only the fingertips of one hand. Using both hands, or the whole hand, leads to sticky pastry. The warmth of the fingertips is important for softening the fat, but once that is done, mixing and kneading should be as light and quick as possible. The pastry can be brought together very quickly by using a palette knife. Because of the high proportion of fat, no water is added.

Modern processors enable the most unskilled cook to make these pastries in seconds. Simply put all the ingredients (the fat in smallish pieces) into the machine and process until the paste forms a ball. This may take a minute or so. The mixture first becomes crumbly, then as it warms up the butter softens and largish lumps appear. When these are gathered into one or two cohesive lumps the paste is made. Do not over-process as the paste will become sticky and taste greasy. The speed of the processor makes for very good pastry.These pastries become crisp as they cool. When biscuit coloured and cooked they will feel soft in the centre. When completely cool, slide off the baking sheet using a palette knife.

HOT WATERCRUST. This is made by heating water and fat together and mixing them into the flour. Because of the high proportion of water, this pastry is inclined to be hard. Its strength and firmness allows it to encase heavy mixtures, such as an English pork pie, without collapsing. Also, as the fat used is generally lard, the pastry can lack flavour, so add a good spoon of salt. Many old recipes recommend throwing the pastry away uneaten once it has done its duty as container.

Do not allow the water to boil before the fat has melted. If the water reduces by boiling, the proportion of water to flour will not be correct. Quickly mix the water and melted fat into the flour in a warm bowl, then keep it covered with a hot damp cloth. This prevents the fat from becoming set and the pastry from flaking and drying out.

CHOUX PASTRY. Like Yorkshire pudding batter, this pastry contains water and eggs and depends on the rising of the steam within it to produce a puffy, hollow pastry case. It is easy to make if the recipe is followed closely. The following points are particularly important:

1. Measure ingredients exactly. Proportions are important with choux.

2. Do not allow the water to boil until the butter has melted, but when it has, bring it immediately to a full rolling boil. Boiling the water too soon will cause too much evaporation.

3. Have the sifted flour ready in a bowl so that the minute the rolling boil is achieved, you can tip in the flour, all in one go.

4. Beat fast and vigorously to get rid of lumps before they cook hard.

5. Do not over-beat. Stop once the mixture is leaving the sides of the pan.

6. Cool slightly before adding egg, otherwise the egg will scramble.

7. Do not beat in more egg than is necessary to achieve a dropping consistency. If the mixture is too stiff, the pastry will be stodgy. If it is too thin, it will rise unevenly into shapeless lumps.

8. Bake until it is a good, even brown, otherwise the inside of the pastry will be uncooked.

9. If the pastry is to be served cold, split the buns/rings, or poke a hole in each of them with a skewer, to allow the steam inside to escape. If steam remains trapped inside, the pastry will be soggy and a little heavy. Opened-up pastry or small buns with holes in them can be returned to the oven, hole uppermost, to dry out further.

10. Serve the pastry on the day it is made (or store frozen), as it stales rapidly and does not keep well in a tin. See page 129 for chocolate profiteroles recipe.

FLAKY PASTRY AND PUFF PASTRY. These are begun rather like the first stage for preparing shortcrust pastry, though the consistency is initially softer and less 'short', as they contain a high proportion of water. Then more fat, either in a solid block or in small pieces, is incoporated into the paste, which is rolled, folded and re-rolled several times. This process creates layers of pastry which, in the heat of the oven, will rise into light thin leaves. For instance, puff pastry, which is folded in three and rolled out six times, will have 729 layers.

As the whole aim is to create the layers without allowing the incorporated fat to melt, start with everything cool, including the bowl, the ingredients and even the worktop if possible. Short, quick strokes (rather than long steady ones) allow the bubbles of air so carefully incorporated in the pastry to move about while the fat is gradually and evenly distributed in the paste. Work lightly and do not stretch the paste, for the layers you have built up will tear and allow the air and fat to escape. Chill the pastry between rollings or at any point if there is a danger of the fat breaking through the pastry, or if the pastry becomes sticky and warm. It sounds like a complicated business, but it is a lot easier done than said: follow the instructions on page 91 (puff pastry), page 90 (rough puff pastry) and page 90 (flaky pastry).

Pastry rises evenly to a crisp crust in a steamy atmosphere. For this reason flaky and puff pastries (which are expected to rise in the oven) are sometimes baked with a roasting tin full of water at the bottom of the oven, or on a wet baking sheet. The oven temperature is set high to cause rapid expansion of the trapped layers of air and quick cooking of the dough before the fat has time to melt and run out.

STRUDEL PASTRY. This differs from most other pastries in that it actually benefits from heavy handling. It is beaten and stretched, thumped and kneaded. This treatment allows the gluten to expand and promotes elasticity in the dough. The paste is rolled and stretched on a cloth (the bigger the better) until it is so thin that you should be able to read fine print through it. Keep the paste covered and moist when not in use. When the pastry is pulled out, brush it with butter or oil to prevent it cracking and drying, or keep it covered with a damp cloth. Strudel pastry can be bought in ready-rolled leaves from specialist food shops, especially Greek-owned ones. Called 'phyllo' or 'filo' pastry, it is used to make the Middle Eastern baklava. Detailed instructions for strudel pastry appear on page 94.

Shortcrust Pastry (Pâte Brisée)

170g/6oz plain flour
pinch of salt
30g/1oz lard
55g/2oz butter
very cold water

1. Sift the flour with the salt.

2. Rub in the fats until the mixture looks like coarse breadcrumbs.

3. Add 30ml/2 tablespoons water to the mixture. Mix to a firm dough, first with a knife, and finally with one hand. It may be necessary to add more water, but the pastry should not be too damp. (Though crumbly pastry is more difficult to handle, it produces a shorter, lighter result.)

4. Chill, wrapped, for 30 minutes before using. Or allow to relax after rolling out but before baking.

Rich Shortcrust Pastry

170g/6oz plain flour
pinch of salt
100g/3^1/$_2$oz butter
1 egg yolk
very cold water

1. Sift the flour with the salt.

2. Rub in the butter until the mixture looks like breadcrumbs.

3. Mix the yolk with 30ml/2 tablespoons water and add to the mixture.

4. Mix to a firm dough, first with a knife, and finally with one hand. It may be necessary to add more water, but the pastry should not be too damp. (Though crumbly pastry is more difficult to handle, it produces a shorter, lighter result.)

5. Chill, wrapped, for 30 minutes before using, or allow to relax after rolling out but before baking.

NOTE: To make sweet rich shortcrust pastry, mix in 15ml/1 tablespoon caster sugar once the fat has been rubbed into the flour.

Sweet Pastry

170g/6oz plain flour
large pinch of salt
2.5ml/$^1/_2$ teaspoon baking powder
100g/3$^1/_2$ oz unsalted butter
55g/2oz caster sugar
1 egg yolk
55ml/2 fl oz double cream

1. Sift the flour, salt and baking powder into a large bowl.

2. Rub in the butter until the mixture looks like coarse breadcrumbs. Stir in the sugar.

3. Mix the egg yolk with the cream and add to the mixture.

4. Mix to a firm dough, first with a knife and finally with one hand. Chill, wrapped, for 30 minutes before using, or allow to relax after rolling out but before baking.

Pâte Sablée

285g/10oz flour
pinch of salt
225g/8oz butter, softened
110g/4oz icing sugar, sifted
2 egg yolks
2 drops vanilla essence

1. Sift the flour on to a board with the salt. Make a large well in the centre and put the butter in it. Place the egg yolks and sugar on the butter with the vanilla essence.

2. Using the fingertips of one hand, 'peck' the butter, yolks and sugar together. When mixed to a soft paste, draw in the flour and knead lightly until the pastry is just smooth.

3. If the pastry is very soft, chill before rolling or pressing out to the required shape. In any event the pastry must be allowed to relax for 30 minutes before baking, either before or after rolling out.

Suet Pastry

As suet pastry is most often used for steamed puddings, instructions for lining a pudding basin are included here.

butter for greasing
340g/12oz self-raising flour
salt
170g/6oz shredded beef suet
water to mix

1. Grease a 1.1 litre/2 pint pudding basin.

2. Sift the flour with a good pinch of salt into a bowl. Stir in the shredded suet and add enough water to mix, first with a knife, and then with one hand, to a soft dough.

3. On a floured surface, roll out two-thirds of the pastry into a round about 1cm/ $^1/_2$ inch thick. Sprinkle the pastry evenly with flour.

4. Fold the round in half and place the open curved sides towards you.

5. Shape the pastry by rolling the straight edge away from you and gently pushing the middle and pulling the sides to form a bag that, when spread out, will fit the pudding basin.

6. With a dry pastry brush, remove all excess flour and place the bag in the well-greased basin.

7. Fill the pastry bag with the desired mixture.

8. Roll out the remaining piece of pastry and use it as a lid, damping the edges and pressing them firmly together.

9. Cover the basin with buttered greaseproof paper, pleated in the centre, and a layer of pleated tin foil. (Pleating the paper and foil allows the pastry to expand slightly without bursting the wrappings.) Tie down firmly to prevent water or steam getting in during cooking.

NOTE: Occasionally suet pastry is used for other purposes than steamed puddings, in which case it should be mixed as above and then handled like any other pastry, except that it does not need to relax before cooking.

Wholemeal Pastry

140g/5oz butter
110g/4oz wholemeal flour
110g/4oz plain flour
pinch of salt
water

1. Rub the butter into the flours and salt until the mixture looks like coarse breadcrumbs.

2. Add 30ml/2 tablespoons water to the mixture.

3. Mix to a firm dough, first with a knife and then with one hand. It may be necessary to add more water, but the pastry should not be too damp. (Although crumbly pastry is more difficult to handle, it produces a shorter, lighter result.)

4. Chill in the refrigerator for at least 30 minutes before using, or allow the rolled-out pastry to relax before baking.

NOTE I: To make sweet wholemeal pastry, mix in 30ml/2 tablespoons sugar once the fat has been rubbed into the flour.

NOTE II: All wholemeal flour may be used if preferred.

Herby Wholemeal Pastry

110g/4oz plain flour
110g/4oz wholemeal flour
a pinch of salt
110g/4oz butter, chopped
15ml/1 tablespoon chopped thyme
water

1. Sift the flours with the salt and put any bran caught in the sieve back into the flour.

2. Rub the butter into the flour until the mixture looks like coarse breadcrumbs. Add the thyme.

3. Add enough water to the mixture and mix first with a knife and then with one hand to a firm dough. Chill in the refrigerator for 10 minutes and use as required.

Rough Puff Pastry

225g/8oz plain flour
pinch of salt
140g/5oz butter
very cold water

1. Sift the flour and salt into a cold bowl.
Cut the butter into knobs about the size of
a sugar lump and add to the flour. Do not
rub in but add enough water to just bind
the paste together. Mix first with a knife,
then with one hand. Knead very lightly.
Then wrap the pastry up and leave to relax
for 10 minutes in the refrigerator.

2. On a floured board, roll the pastry into a
strip about 30 x 10cm/12 x 4 inches long.
This must be done carefully: with a heavy
rolling pin, press firmly on the pastry and
give short sharp rolls until the pastry has
reached the required size. The surface of
the pastry should not be over-stretched
and broken.

3. Fold the strip into 3 and turn so that the
folded edge is to your left, like a closed
book. Again roll out into a strip 1cm/
$^1/_2$ inch thick. Fold in 3 again and leave,
wrapped, in the refrigerator for 15 minutes.

4. Roll and fold the pastry as before, then
chill again for 15 minutes.

5. Roll and fold again, by which time the
pastry should be ready for use, with no
signs of streakiness.

6. Roll into the required shape. Then chill
again before baking.

Flaky Pastry

225g/8oz plain flour
pinch of salt
85g/3oz butter
85g/3oz lard
150ml/$^1/_4$ pint cold water

1. Sift the flour with a pinch of salt. Rub in
half the butter. Add enough cold water to
mix with a knife to a doughy consistency.
Turn out on to a floured board and knead
until just smooth. Roll into an oblong
about 10 x 30cm/4 x 12 inches long.
Cut half the lard into tiny pieces and dot
them evenly all over the top two-thirds of
the pastry, leaving a good margin.

2. Fold the pastry in 3, folding first the
unlarded third up, then the larded top third
down and pressing the edges to seal them.
Give a 90-degree anti-clockwise turn so that
the folded closed edge is to your left. Then
repeat the rolling and folding process
(without adding any fat).

3. Roll out again, dot with the remaining
butter as before, and fold and seal as before.
Then repeat using the rest of the lard.

4. Fold, wrap the pastry and 'relax' (or
chill) for 10-15 minutes. Then roll and fold
once again (without adding any fat) and
then use as required.

NOTE: As a general rule, flaky pastry is
rolled out thinly, and baked at about
220°C/425°F/gas mark 7. If it becomes too
warm, sticky and difficult to handle,
wrap it up and chill it for 15 minutes.

Puff Pastry

225g/8oz plain flour
pinch of salt
30g/1oz lard
150ml/¹/₄ pint icy water
140-200g/5-7oz butter

1. If you have never made puff pastry before, use the smaller amount of butter: this will give a normal pastry. If you have some experience, more butter will produce a lighter, very rich pastry.

2. Sift the flour with a pinch of salt. Rub in the lard. Add the icy water and mix with a knife to a doughy consistency. Turn on to the table and knead quickly until just smooth. Wrap in polythene or a cloth and leave in the refrigerator for 30 minutes to relax.

3. Lightly flour the table top or board and roll the dough into a rectangle about 10 x 30cm/4 x 12 inches long.

4. Tap the butter lightly with a floured rolling pin to get it into a flattened block about 9 x 8cm/3¹/₂ x 3 inches. Put the butter on the rectangle of pastry and fold both ends over to enclose it. Fold the third closest to you over first and then bring the top third down. Press the sides together to prevent the butter escaping. Give it a 90-degree anti-clockwise turn so that the folded, closed edge is on your left.

5. Now tap the pastry parcel with the rolling pin to flatten the butter a little; then roll out, quickly and lightly, until the pastry is 3 times as long as it is wide. Fold it very evenly in 3, first folding the third closest to you over, then bringing the top third down. Give it a 90-degree anti-clockwise turn so that the folded, closed edge is on your left. Again press the edges firmly with the rolling pin. Then roll out again to form a rectangle as before.

6. Now the pastry has had 2 rolls and folds, or 'turns' as they are called. It should be put to rest in a cool place for 30 minutes or so. The rolling and folding must be repeated twice more, the pastry again rested, and then again given 2 more 'turns'. This makes a total of 6 turns. If the butter is still very streaky, roll and fold it once more.

Martha Stewart's Walnut Pastry

225g/8oz plain flour
pinch of salt
110g/4oz butter
140g/5oz ground walnuts
45g/1¹/₂ oz sugar
beaten egg

1. Sift the flour and salt into a bowl. Rub in the butter until the mixture resembles coarse breadcrumbs. Add the walnuts.

2. Stir in the sugar and add enough beaten egg (probably half an egg) to just bind the mixture together. Knead lightly.
Chill before use.

NOTE: If you have a food processor, simply beat all the ingredients together until lightly combined. Chill before use.

Bouchée Cases

MAKES ABOUT 20
puff pastry made with 225g/8oz flour (see
page 91)
beaten egg

1. Set the oven to 220°C/425°F/gas mark 7.

2. Roll out the pastry to 5mm/¹/₄ inch. With a 4cm/1¹/₂ inch round pastry cutter, stamp it out in rounds. With a slightly smaller cutter, cut a circle in the centre of each round, but be careful not to stamp the pastry more than halfway through.

3. Brush the tops with beaten egg, taking care not to get egg on the sides, which would prevent the pastry layers separating and rising.

4. Bake on a wet baking sheet until brown and crisp; about 12 minutes.

5. Take off the pastry 'lids' and scrape out any raw pastry left inside. Return the bouchée cases to the oven for 4 minutes to dry out. Cool on a wire rack.

NOTE: Bouchée cases, if they are to be eaten hot, should either be filled while they are still very hot with a cooked hot filling, or (if they are cooked and cold) with a cooked cold filling. Hot fillings will tend to make the pastry soggy during the reheating process. If both filling and pastry go into the oven cold, the pastry will have time to become crisp again before the filling is hot.

Vol-au-Vents

MAKES 1 OR 2
*puff pastry made with 225g/8oz flour (see
   page 91)*
beaten egg
salt

1. Set the oven to 220°C/425°F/gas mark 7.

2. Roll the pastry to 1cm/^{1}/$_2$ inch thickness
and cut into a round about the size of a
dessert plate. Place on a wet baking sheet.
Using a cutter half the size of the pastry
round, cut into the centre of the pastry,
but take care not to cut right through to the
baking sheet.

3. Flour the blade of a knife and use this to
'knock up' the sides of the pastry: try to
slightly separate the leaves of the pastry
horizontally; this means that the edge will
flake readily when cooking. (It counteracts
the squashing effect of the cutter used to
cut out the round, which may have pressed
the edges together, making it more difficult
for the pastry to rise in even layers.)

4. Mix a pinch of salt into the beaten egg.
Brush the pastry carefully with this egg
wash, avoiding the knocked-up sides;
if they are covered with egg, the pastry
will not rise.

5. With the back of the knife blade, make a
star pattern on the borders of the vol-au-
vent case and mark a lattice pattern on the
inner circle. (The back rather than the
sharp edge of the blade is used as this will
not cut into the pastry; the idea is to make
a pattern without cutting through the
surface of the pastry.)

6. Bake in a hot oven for 30 minutes, and
carefully lift off the top of the inner circle.
Keep this for the lid of the case when
filled. Pull out and discard any partially
cooked pastry from the centre of the case.

7. Return the case to the oven for 2 minutes
to dry out. The vol-au-vent is now ready
for filling. Ideally the heated pastry case is
filled with hot filling, and then served.

NOTE: Flaky or rough puff pastry are also
suitable. But the method of cutting is
different: cut the pastry into 2 rounds the
size of a side plate. Stamp a circle right out
of the centre of one of them. Brush the
uncut round with egg and place the ring of
pastry on top. Bake the middle small
round of pastry too, and use it for the vol-
au-vent lid.

Filo or Strudel Pastry

285g/10oz plain flour
pinch of salt
1 egg
150ml/¼ pint water
5ml/1 teaspoon oil

1. Sift the flour and salt into a bowl.

2. Beat the egg and add the water and oil. First with a knife and then with one hand, mix the water and egg into the flour, adding more water if necessary to make a soft dough.

3. The paste now has to be beaten: lift the whole mixture up in one hand and then, with a flick of the wrist, slap it on to a lightly floured board. Continue doing this until the paste no longer sticks to your fingers, and the whole mixture is smooth and very elastic. Put it into a clean floured bowl. Cover and leave in a warm place for 15 minutes.

4. The pastry is now ready for rolling and pulling. To do this, flour a tea towel or large cloth on a table top and roll out the pastry as thinly as you can. Now put your hand (well floured) under the pastry and, keeping your hand fairly flat, gently stretch and pull the pastry, gradually and carefully working your way round until the paste is paper thin. (You should be able to see through it easily.) Trim off the thick edges.

5. Use immediately, as strudel pastry dries

out and cracks very quickly. Brushing with melted butter or oil helps to prevent this. Or the pastry sheets may be kept covered with a damp cloth.

NOTE: If the paste is not for immediate use wrap it well and keep refrigerated (for up to three days) or frozen. Flour the pastry surfaces before folding up. This will prevent sticking.

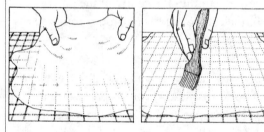

Stretch and pull until almost transparent; brush with butter.

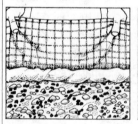

Fill as required (see page 135), roll up (using the tea towel).

Choux Pastry

85g/3oz butter
220ml/7 fl oz water
105g/3³/4 oz plain flour, well sifted
pinch of salt
3 eggs

1. Put the butter and water together in a heavy saucepan. Bring slowly to the boil so that by the time the water boils the butter is completely melted.

2. Immediately the mixture is boiling really fast, tip in all the flour and draw the pan off the heat.

3. Working as fast as you can, beat the mixture hard with a wooden spoon: it will soon become thick and smooth and leave the sides of the pan. Beat in the salt.

4. Stand the bottom of the saucepan in a basin or sink of cold water to speed up the cooling process.

5. When the mixture is cool, beat in the eggs, a little at at time, until it is soft, shiny and smooth. If the eggs are large, it may not be necessary to add all of them. The mixture should be of a dropping consistency – not too runny. ('Dropping consistency' means that the mixture will fall off a spoon rather reluctantly and all in a blob; if it runs off, it is too wet, and if it will not fall off even when the spoon is jerked slightly, it is too thick.)

6. Use as required.

Pâte Sucrée

170g/6oz plain flour
pinch of salt
85g/3oz butter, softened
3 egg yolks
85g/3oz sugar
2 drops vanilla essence

1. Sift the flour on to a board with a pinch of salt. Make a large well in the centre and put the butter in it. Place the egg yolks and sugar on the butter with the vanilla essence.

2. Using the fingertips of one hand, mix the butter, yolks and sugar together. When mixed to a soft paste, draw in the flour and knead until the pastry is just smooth.

3. If the pastry is very soft, chill before rolling or pressing out to the required shape. In any event the pastry must be allowed to relax for 30 minutes either before or after rolling out, but before baking.

Almond Pastry (Pâte Frollée)

Care must be taken when making this because if it is over-kneaded the oil will run from the almonds, resulting in an oily paste.

110g/4oz plain flour
pinch of salt
45g/1¹/2 oz ground almonds
45g/1¹/2 oz caster sugar
1 egg yolk or beaten egg
2 drops vanilla essence
85g/3oz butter, softened

1. Sift the flour with the salt on to a board or table top. Scatter over the ground almonds. Make a large well in the centre and put in the sugar, beaten egg or yolk and vanilla essence.

2. Using one hand only, mix the egg and sugar with your fingertips. When creamy, add the softened butter and continue to mix, gradually drawing in the flour and almonds.

3. Knead gently to a paste and chill. Allow to relax for 30 minutes before baking.

Pâte à Pâté

225g/8oz plain flour
2.5ml/¹/2 teaspoon salt
165g/5¹/2 oz butter, softened
2 small egg yolks
up to 30ml/2 tablespoons water

1. Sift the flour and salt on to the table top. Make a large well in the centre and put the butter and yolks in it. Work the yolks and butter together with the fingers of one hand and draw in the surrounding flour, adding the water to give a soft, malleable, but not sticky paste.

2. Wrap and leave to rest in the refrigerator for 30 minutes. Use as required.

Breads

Black Bun

Old-Fashioned Boiled Christmas Cake

Left: Gâteau Nougatine. Above: Scones.

Biscuits

Mince Pies

Above: Individual Apple Charlottes. Right: Individual Apple Tarts.

Left: Charlotte's Higgledy Piggledy Tart. Above: Tarte Tatin

Poached Pear and Polenta Tart

Gâteau Pithiviers

Left: Sablé aux Fraises. Above: Aubergine and Chestnut Pie.

Cheese Soufflé

Hot Watercrust Pastry

This pastry is used for raised pies, such as pork pie and game pie.

225g/8oz plain flour
2.5ml/¹/2 teaspoon salt
1 beaten egg
100ml/3¹/2 fl oz water
38g/1¹/4 oz butter
38g/1¹/4 oz lard

1. Wrap a piece of paper around the outside of a wide jar or small straight-sided saucepan. The paper can be held in position by tucking it in the opening of the jar or saucepan. Leave it upside down while you make the pastry.

2. Sift the flour and salt into a bowl. Make a dip in the middle, break the egg into it and toss a liberal covering of flour over the egg.

3. Put the water, butter and lard into a saucepan and bring slowly to the boil.

4. Once the liquid is boiling, pour it on to the flour, mixing with a knife as you do so.

Knead until all the egg streaks have gone and the pastry is smooth.

5. Wrap in a piece of cling film and leave in the refrigerator for 10 minutes.

6. Reserve about a third of the paste for the lid, keeping it covered or wrapped and in a warm place. Roll out the remaining paste to a circle and drape it over the jar or saucepan. Working fast, shape the pastry to cover the jar or saucepan to a depth of about 7cm/2¹/2 inches. Leave to chill in the refrigerator.

7. As the pastry cools it will harden. When hard, turn the jar or saucepan over and remove it carefully, leaving the paper inside the pastry case. Carefully draw the paper away from the pastry and when it is all loosened take it out. Stand the pastry case on a baking sheet and fill as required. Use the reserved third of the pastry to make the lid, wetting the rim of the pie case to make it stick down well. Bake as required.

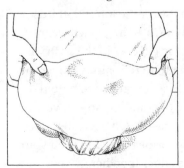

Drape pastry over prepared jar; when cool, remove jar and carefully draw out the paper. Crimp the edges together and bake.

Danish Pastries

Most Danish pastries require almond
filling and icing as well as the basic dough.
Instructions for these are given here, and
the individual instructions for Pinwheels,
Almond Squares etc. are on pages 75, 77-8.

   When rolling out Danish pastry, care
should be taken to prevent the butter
breaking through the paste and making
the resulting pastry heavy. Use a heavy
rolling pin, bring it fairly firmly down on
to the pastry and roll with short, quick,
firm rolls. Do not 'push' it. Avoid using
too much flour. If the paste is becoming
warm and unmanageable, wrap it up and
chill it well before proceeding.

   The icing should not be made until the
pastries are baked. Danish pastries are
frequently scattered with flaked browned
almonds while the icing is still wet.
Sometimes sultanas, small pieces of tinned
pineapple or apple purée are included in
the filling.

MAKES 6
For the pastry:
15g/¹/2 oz fresh yeast
15ml/1 tablespoon caster sugar
100ml/3 fl oz milk, warmed
225g/8oz plain flour
pinch of salt
1 egg, lightly beaten
110g/4oz unsalted butter, softened

For the almond paste filling:
45g/1¹/2 oz butter
45g/1¹/2 oz icing sugar
30g/1oz ground almonds
2 drops vanilla essence

For the glaze:
1 egg, beaten

For the glacé icing:
110g/4oz icing sugar
boiling water to mix

1. Dissolve the yeast with 15ml/1 teaspoon
of the sugar and the milk.

2. Sift the flour with a pinch of salt into a
warmed bowl. Add the remaining sugar.
Make a well in the centre and drop into it
the egg and the yeast mixture.

3. Using a round-bladed knife, mix the
liquids, gradually drawing in the
surrounding flour to make a soft dough.
If extra liquid is required, add a little more
water.

4. When the dough leaves the sides of the
bowl, turn it on to a floured surface and
bring together gently until fairly smooth.
Roll into a longish rectangle 5mm/¹/4 inch
thick.

5. Divide the butter into hazelnut-sized
pieces and dot it over the top two-thirds of
the dough, leaving a 1cm/¹/2 inch clear
margin round the edge. Fold the pastry in
3, folding the unbuttered third up over the
centre section first, and then the buttered
top third down over it. You now have a
thick 'parcel' of pastry. Give it a 90-degree
turn so that the former top edge is on your
right. Press the edges together.

6. Dust lightly with flour and roll into a long rectangle again. Fold in 3 as before. Chill for 15 minutes.

7. Roll and fold the pastry once or twice again, turning it in the same direction as before, until the butter is worked in well and the paste does not look streaky. Chill for at least 30 minutes or overnight, before proceeding with one of the recipes on pages 75, 77-8.

8. To make the almond paste, cream the butter, add the sugar and beat well until light and soft. Mix in the ground almonds and flavour with vanilla essence. Mix well but do not overbeat or the oil will run from the almonds, making the paste greasy.

9. When ready to use the glacé icing: mix enough boiling water into the sugar to give an icing that will run fairly easily – about the consistency of cream.

NOTE: If using dried yeast or easy-blend see page 12.

Anchovy Puff Pastry Fingers

MAKES 40
*rough puff pastry made with 225g/8oz flour
  (see page 90)*
40 anchovy fillets (about 1 tin)
90ml/6 tablespoons milk
beaten egg

1. Divide the pastry into two and roll each piece thinly to a rectangle 30 x 10cm/12 x 4 inches. Slide on to 2 baking sheets and put in the refrigerator to relax.

2. Soak the anchovies in milk for 15 minutes to remove any oil and excess salt. Drain and trim the fillets neatly. Heat the oven to 200°C/400°F/gas mark 6.

3. Brush one piece of pastry with beaten egg, prick with a fork and place the anchovy fillets neatly on it. You should be able to lay out 2 neat rows of 20 fillets in each row.

4. Cover with the second piece of pastry and brush again with egg wash. Press well together and prick all over with a fork.

5. Bake in the oven for 10-12 minutes until golden brown. Leave to cool on a wire rack.

6. When cold, cut the pastry into neat fingers of 5 x 1cm/2 x $^1/_2$ inch in such a way that each finger has an anchovy fillet sandwiched inside it

7. Warm through before serving.

Twisted Cheese Straws

MAKES 50

170g/6oz plain flour
pinch of salt
100g/3¹/2 oz butter
45g/1¹/2oz grated Parmesan or mixed
  Parmesan and Gruyère or Cheddar cheese
pinch of pepper
pinch of cayenne pepper
pinch of dry English mustard
beaten egg

1. Set the oven to 190°C/375°F/gas mark 5.

2. Sift the flour into a basin with a pinch of salt. Rub the butter into the flour with your fingertips until the mixture resembles fine breadcrumbs. Add the grated cheese and seasonings.

3. Bind the mixture together with enough egg to make a stiff dough. Refrigerate for 10 minutes.

4. Line a baking sheet with greaseproof paper. Roll the paste into a rectangle and cut into strips 9 x 2cm/3¹/2 x ³/4 inch. Twist each strip 2-3 times like a barley sugar stick. Bake for 8-10 minutes. They should be a biscuit brown.

Spinach and Ricotta Strudels

MAKES 20

225g/8oz frozen chopped spinach
110g/4oz butter
110g/4oz ricotta cheese
salt and freshly ground black pepper
good pinch of grated nutmeg
4 sheets filo pastry
1 egg, beaten

1. Set the oven to 200°C/400°F/gas mark 6.

2. Defrost the spinach. Melt 30g/1oz of the butter and add the spinach, ricotta and seasonings.

3. Melt the remaining butter and brush it over the sheets of filo pastry.

4. Cut each sheet of pastry into strips 5cm/2 inches wide.

5. Place a spoonful of filling at one end of each strip. Form a triangle by folding the right-hand corner to the opposite side, and fold over and then across from the left-hand corner to the right edge. Continue folding until the strip of pastry is used up.

6. Brush the strudels with beaten egg. Place on a greased baking sheet and bake for about 10 minutes or until golden brown.

Sausage Rolls

MAKES 12
400g/14oz sausagemeat
30g/1oz chopped parsley
30g/1oz chopped onion
salt and pepper
shortcrust pastry made with 225g/8oz flour
  (see page 86)
1 egg, beaten

1. Set the oven to 200°C/400°F/gas mark 6.

2. Mix together the sausagemeat, parsley, onion and seasonings.

3. Roll out the pastry to a large rectangle about 0.25cm/^{1}/$_8$ inch thick and cut in half lengthways.

4. With wet hands, roll the meat mixture into 2 long sausages the same length as the pastry and place one down the centre of each piece.

5. Damp one edge of each strip and bring the pastry over the sausagemeat, pressing the edges together and making sure that the join is underneath the roll.

6. Brush with beaten egg. Cut into 5cm/2 inch lengths. Using a pair of scissors, snip a small 'V' in the top of each sausage roll. (This is to allow steam to escape during cooking. A couple of small diagonal slashes made with a sharp knife will do as well.)

7. Place on a baking sheet and bake for 25-30 minutes.

Eccles Cakes

MAKES 6
rough puff pastry made with 225g/8oz flour
  (see page 90)
15g/^{1}/$_2$ oz butter
55g/2oz brown sugar
110g/4oz currants
30g/1oz chopped mixed peel
2.5ml/^{1}/$_2$ teaspoon ground cinnamon
1.25ml/^{1}/$_4$ teaspoon ground nutmeg
1.25ml/^{1}/$_4$ teaspoon ground ginger
grated rind of ^{1}/$_2$ lemon
5ml/1 teaspoon lemon juice

For the glaze:
1 egg white
caster sugar

1. Set the oven to 220°C/425°F/gas mark 7. Roll the pastry to the thickness of a coin. Cut out rounds 12.5cm/5 inches in diameter. Put aside to relax. Melt the butter in a pan and stir in all the other filling ingredients. Cool.

2. Place a good teaspoon of filling in the centre of each pastry round. Damp the edges of the pastry and press together in the centre, forming a small ball. Turn the balls over and lightly roll them until the fruit begins to show through the pastry.

3. With a sharp knife, make 3 small parallel cuts on the top. Lightly beat the egg white with a fork. Brush the top of the cakes with this and sprinkle with caster sugar.

4. Place on a wet baking sheet and bake for 20 minutes or until lightly browned.

Flat Ham Pie

SERVES 6

pâte à pâté made with 450g/1lb flour (see page 96)
55g/2oz Gruyère or Cheddar cheese, grated
30g/1oz grated Parmesan
45g/1¹/₂oz butter, melted
55g/2oz fresh white breadcrumbs
225g/8oz ham
30ml/2 tablespoons chopped dill or chives
1 large garlic clove, crushed
150ml/¹/₄ pint soured cream
freshly ground black pepper
juice of ¹/₂ lemon
beaten egg

1. Make up the pâte à pâté and roll out into rectangles, one to fit a Swiss roll tin, the other slightly larger.

2. Set the oven to 200°C/400°F/gas mark 6.

3. Lightly grease and flour the back of a Swiss roll tin or a rectangular baking sheet. Put the smaller rectangle of pastry on it and prick all over with a fork. Bake for 15 minutes and leave to cool.

4. Mix together the Gruyère or Cheddar, the Parmesan, the melted butter and the breadcrumbs. Scatter half of this all over the half-cooked pastry, leaving a good 1cm/¹/₂ inch clear all round the edge.

5. Chop the ham into small pieces and scatter it on top of the cheese mixture. Then scatter over the dill or chives.

6. Mix the garlic with the soured cream and spread all over the ham. Season well with pepper but no salt.

7. Sprinkle evenly with the lemon juice and top with the rest of the cheese mixture. Wet the edge of the bottom piece of pastry with lightly beaten egg and put the top sheet of pastry in place, pressing the edges to seal it well.

8. Use any pastry trimmings to decorate the pie and brush all over with the beaten egg.

9. Bake until the pastry is crisp and pale brown. Serve hot or cold.

LIGHT RED/ROSE

Puddings

Chocolate Roulade

SERVES 6
5 eggs
140g/5oz caster sugar
225g/8oz dark sweetened chocolate, roughly
  chopped
75ml/3 fl oz water
5ml/1 teaspoon strong instant coffee
290ml/¹/2 pint double cream
icing sugar

To prepare the tin:
oil, flour, caster sugar

1. Take a large roasting pan and cut a double layer of greaseproof paper slightly bigger than it. Lay this in the tin; don't worry if the edges stick up untidily round the sides. Brush the paper lightly with oil and sprinkle with flour and then caster sugar. Set the oven to 200°C/400°F/gas mark 6.

2. Separate the eggs and beat the yolks and the sugar until pale and mousse-like.

3. Put the chocolate, water and coffee into a thick-bottomed saucepan and melt over a gentle heat. Stir into the yolk mixture.

4. Whisk the whites until stiff but not dry. With a metal spoon, stir a small amount thoroughly into the chocolate mixture, to 'loosen' it. Fold the rest of the whites in gently. Spread the mixture evenly on the paper.

5. Bake for about 12 minutes until the top is slightly browned and firm to touch.

6. Slide the cake and paper out of the roasting pan on to a wire rack. Cover immediately with a damp tea towel (to prevent the cake from cracking) and leave to cool, preferably overnight.

7. Whip the cream and spread it evenly over the cake. Roll up like a Swiss roll, removing the paper as you go. Put the roll on to a serving dish and, just before serving, sift a little icing sugar over the top.

NOTE I: The cake is very moist and inclined to break apart. But it doesn't matter. Just stick it together with the cream when rolling up. The last-minute sifted icing sugar will do wonders for the appearance.

NOTE II: If this cake is used as a Yule log the tendency to crack is a positive advantage: do not cover with a tea towel when leaving overnight. Before filling, flip the whole flat cake over on to a tea towel. Carefully peel off the backing paper, then fill with cream and roll up. The firm skin will crack very like the bark of a tree. Sprigs of holly or marzipan toadstools help to give a festive look. A dusting of icing sugar will look like snow.

FORTIFIED SWEET WHITE

Hazelnut Roulade

SERVES 4-6
3 eggs
55g/2oz caster sugar
15ml/1 tablespoon plain flour
1.25ml/¹/4 teaspoon baking powder
55g/2oz browned ground hazelnuts
icing sugar
150ml/¹/4 pint double cream, whipped

1. Set the oven to 180°C/350°F/gas mark 4.

2. Prepare a paper case as for a Swiss roll.
It should be the size of a piece of A4 paper.
Grease it lightly.

3. Separate the eggs and beat the yolks and
the sugar together until pale and mousse-
like.

4. Sift the flour with the baking powder
and fold it into the egg-yolk mixture along
with the nuts.

5. Whisk the egg whites until stiff but not
dry and fold into the mixture.

6. Spread the mixture into the prepared
paper case.

7. Bake for about 20 minutes until the top
is slightly browned and firm to touch.

8. Remove the roulade from the oven and
allow to cool, covered with a sheet of
kitchen paper.

9. Sprinkle icing sugar on to a piece of
greaseproof paper and turn the roulade on

to it. Remove the original piece of paper.

10. Spread the whipped cream evenly over
the roulade and roll it up like a Swiss roll.

NOTE: Serve the hazelnut roulade with a
raspberry coulis, or add fresh fruit to the
cream before rolling up the roulade.

RICH SWEET WHITE

Apple Charlottes

SERVES 4
55g/2oz granulated sugar
5 dessert apples, e.g. Discovery or Cox,
  peeled, cored and sliced
30ml/2 tablespoons Calvados
juice of 1 orange
pinch of ground cinnamon
70g/2¹⁄₂oz butter
8 slices white bread, crustless

For the sauce:
55g/2oz granulated sugar
grated rind of 1 orange
15ml/1 tablespoon Calvados
55g/2oz butter, cut into small pieces

1. Put the sugar into a heavy saucepan with 2 tablespoons of water and place over a low heat. The sugar should dissolve slowly and become lightly caramelized.

2. Add the apples to the caramel, stir and then add the Calvados, the orange juice, cinnamon and all but 15g/¹⁄₂oz of the butter. Simmer together for 2 minutes.

3. Set the oven to 200°C/400°F/gas mark 6.

4. Butter 4 ramekin dishes using most of the reserved butter.

5. Flatten the bread slightly with a rolling pin. Cut out 8 rounds and use 4 of the rounds to line the base of the ramekins. Use the rest of the bread to line the sides.

6. Drain the apple filling (but reserve the strained liquor) and pile the apple slices into the lined ramekins. Cover with the remaining rounds of bread, buttered on both sides.

7. Put the ramekins on to a baking tray and bake for 15-20 minutes.

8. Meanwhile, prepare the sauce: reduce the apple liquor, by boiling rapidly, to 150ml/¹⁄₄ pint. Set aside.

9. Put the sugar with 2 tablespoons of water into a heavy saucepan, and place over a low heat. Allow the sugar to dissolve and then caramelize. When lightly browned add the reduced apple juice, the orange rind and Calvados. Simmer for 1 minute and gradually whisk in the butter pieces.

10. To serve, turn the Apple Charlottes out on to individual plates and serve with the caramel sauce.

SWEET WHITE

Plum Pie

This recipe leaves the stones in the plums – if preferred, the plums can be cut in half and stoned. If the plums are large or not very ripe they should be pre-cooked in a little sugar syrup before they are baked.

SERVES 6
225g/8oz plain flour
pinch of salt
55g/2oz lard
85g/3oz butter
30-45ml/2-3 tablespoons cold water
caster sugar to dredge

For the filling:
675g/1¹/2lb small plums
45ml/3 tablespoons demerara sugar
2.5ml/¹/2 teaspoon ground cinnamon

1. Preheat the oven to 220°C/425°F/gas mark 7.

2. Sift the flour with the salt into a bowl. Rub in the fats until the mixture resembles coarse breadcrumbs.

3. Stir in enough water to bind the paste together. Push together into a ball, wrap up and chill in the refrigerator while you prepare the filling.

4. Wash the plums and place them in a pie dish with the cinnamon and sugar.

5. Roll out the pastry on a floured board. Cut a band of pastry wider than the rim of the pie dish. Wet the rim and press the band on all the way round. Brush with water and lay over the rolled-out pastry. Trim the edges, press them down firmly and mark with a fork or press into a frilly edge with fingers and thumb.

6. Shape the pastry trimmings into leaves. Brush the top of the pie with water and decorate with the leaves. Brush the leaves with water and dredge the whole pie with caster sugar.

7. Cut 1 or 2 small slits in the pastry top to allow the steam to escape. Bake on the top shelf for 25-35 minutes.

RICH SWEET WHITE

Treacle Tart

SERVES 4
110g/4oz plain flour
pinch of salt
55g/2oz butter
10ml/2 teaspoons caster sugar
1 egg yolk
very cold water

For the filling:
120ml/8 tablespoons golden syrup
grated rind of 1/2 lemon and 10ml/2 teaspoons
  of the juice
pinch of ground ginger (optional)
60ml/4 tablespoons fresh white breadcrumbs

1. Set the oven to 190°C/375°F/gas mark 5.

2. Sift the flour with the salt. Rub in the butter until the mixture looks like breadcrumbs. Add the sugar.

3. Mix the yolk with 30ml/2 tablespoons water, and add to the mixture.

4. Mix to a firm dough, first with a knife, and finally with one hand. It may be necessary to add water but the pastry should not be too wet. (Though crumbly pastry is more difficult to handle, it produces a shorter, lighter result.)

5. Roll the pastry out to 5mm/1/4 inch thick, and line a pie plate or flan ring with it. Prick the bottom with a fork – do not prick all the way through the pastry.

6. Heat the syrup with the lemon juice and rind to make it a little runny. Add the ginger if using.

7. Pour half the syrup into the pastry case.

8. Sprinkle with crumbs until they are soaked. Pour in the remaining syrup and sprinkle in the remaining crumbs.

9. Bake for about 30 minutes or until the filling is almost set and the edge of the pastry is brown. The filling should be a little on the soft side if the tart is to be eaten cold because it hardens as it cools. Ideally, serve lukewarm.

SWEET SPARKLING

Peach Pastry Cake

SERVES 6
70g/2¹/₂oz hazelnuts
85g/3oz butter
55g/2oz caster sugar
110g/4oz plain flour
pinch of salt
3 fresh peaches
190ml/¹/₃ pint whipped cream
icing sugar

1. Toast the nuts in a hot oven. When brown, rub in a dry cloth to remove the skins. Cool. Grind the nuts taking care not to overgrind them or they will be oily.

2. Beat the butter and when soft add the sugar and beat until light and fluffy.
Sift the flour with the salt and stir into the mixture with the nuts.

3. Set the oven to 190°C/375°F/gas mark 5. Divide the paste into 3 and press out into thin flat rounds of 15cm/6 inch diameter. Chill for 30 minutes.

4. Place on baking sheets and bake for 10-12 minutes. Cut 1 into 6 portions before it cools. Allow to cool on a wire rack. They will become crisp as they cool.

5. Skin and slice the peaches. Mix the peach slices with the whipped cream. Using half this mixture as a filling, sandwich the 2 whole rounds of biscuit together. Spread the other half of the filling on the top. Set the cut portions of biscuit into the cream mixture, placing each at a slight angle. Dust with icing sugar before serving.

Apple and Orange Crumble

SERVES 4
3 oranges
900g/2lb cooking apples
45ml/3 tablespoons demerara sugar
pinch of cinnamon

For the crumble:
170g/6oz plain flour
pinch of salt
110g/4oz butter
55g/2oz sugar

1. Peel the oranges as you would an apple, with a sharp knife, removing all the pith. Then cut out the orange segments leaving behind the membranes.

2. Peel and core the apples. Cut into thick slices. Mix with the orange segments and their juice. Add the sugar and cinnamon. Tip into an ovenproof dish. Then set the oven to 200°C/400°F/gas mark 6.

3. Sift the flour and salt into a bowl. Rub in the fat and when the mixture resembles coarse breadcrumbs mix in the sugar. Sprinkle it over the apples and oranges.

4. Bake on a hot baking sheet for 45 minutes or until hot and slightly browned on top.

NOTE: If using wholemeal flour for the crumble topping, use 140g/5oz of melted butter. Instead of rubbing it into the flour, mix briskly with a knife.

SWEET WHITE

Lemon Meringue Pie

SERVES 4
170g/6oz plain flour
pinch of salt
100g/3oz butter
5ml/1 teaspoon caster sugar
1 egg yolk
very cold water

For the filling:
30g/1oz cornflour
290ml/1/2 pint milk
30g/1oz sugar
2 egg yolks
grated rind and juice of 1 lemon

For the meringue:
2 egg whites
110g/4oz caster sugar
little extra caster sugar

1. First make the pastry: sift the flour with the salt. Rub in the butter until the mixture looks like breadcrumbs. Add the sugar.

2. Mix the yolk with 30ml/2 tablespoons water. Add this to the mixture.

3. Mix to a firm dough, first with a knife, and finally with one hand. It may be necessary to add more water, but the pastry should not be too wet. (Though crumbly pastry is more difficult to handle, it produces a shorter, lighter result.)

4. Roll out the pastry and use it to line a 20cm/8 inch flan ring. Leave it in the refrigerator for about 30 minutes to relax (this prevents shrinkage during cooking). Heat the oven to 190°C/375°F/gas mark 5. Bake the pastry blind (see note on page 76).

5. Reduce the oven temperature to 170°C/325°F/ gas mark 3.

6. Meanwhile, make the filling: mix the cornflour (which should be very accurately weighed) with a tablespoon of the milk.

7. Heat the remaining milk. Pour this on to the cornflour paste, stir well and return the mixture to the pan. Boil for 3-4 minutes, stirring continuously. Add the sugar.

8. Allow to cool slightly, then beat in the egg yolks, lemon rind and juice.

9. Pour this mixture immediately into the pastry case. Remove the flan ring and return to the oven for 5 minutes to set the filling. Make the meringue: whisk the egg whites until stiff. Add 15ml/1 tablespoon of the caster sugar and whisk again until very stiff and solid.

10. Fold in the remaining sugar. Pile the meringue on to the pie. It is essential to cover the filling completely or the pie will weep. On the other hand, if you have used a small flan ring do not use all the meringue – the pie will be too sweet and may well weep.

11. Dust with a little extra caster sugar.

12. Place in the oven for 5 minutes or until the meringue is a pale biscuit colour.

NOTE I: Lemon curd (see page 153) makes a good alternative to the lemon custard filling.

NOTE II: When making a meringue mixture with a powerful electric mixer, add half the sugar when the whites are stiff. Whisk again until very shiny and then add the remaining sugar and whisk lightly until just incorporated.

Individual Apple Tarts

MAKES 8
rich shortcrust pastry made with 170g/6oz
  flour (see page 86)
4 dessert apples
caster sugar
Calvados
apricot glaze (see page 153)

1. Set the oven to 220°C/425°F/gas mark 7.

2. Make the rich shortcrust pastry. Divide into 8 pieces. Then on a floured work surface, roll out each piece of pastry as thinly as possible. Cut into 12.5cm/5 inch circles, place on a baking sheet and chill for 20 minutes.

3. Peel the apples. Cut in half and carefully remove the cores, using the point of a knife.

4. Slice the apples finely and arrange half an apple on each piece of chilled pastry. Take care to pack the apples tightly to allow for shrinkage during cooking.

5. Sprinkle each tart evenly with 10ml/2 teaspoons caster sugar.

6. Place in the hot oven on the top shelf for 15 minutes or until golden brown. If it is not quite brown, place it under the grill for 1-2 minutes.

7. Sprinkle with a little Calvados and brush with warm apricot glaze.

FORTIFIED SWEET WHITE

Mincemeat Flan

SERVES 8

rich shortcrust pastry made with 225g/8oz
*   flour (see page 86) or pâte sucrée (see*
*   page 95)*
caster sugar

For the filling:
1 small cooking apple
55g/2oz butter
85g/3oz sultanas
85g/3oz raisins
85g/3oz currants
45g/1¹/₂oz mixed peel, chopped
45g/1¹/₂oz chopped almonds
grated rind of large lemon
2.5ml/¹/₂ teaspoon mixed spice
15ml/1 tablespoon brandy
85g/3oz brown sugar
1 banana, chopped

1. Heat the oven to 190°C/375°F/gas
mark 5.

2. Roll the pastry out to 5mm/¹/₄ inch
thick, and line a 25cm/10 inch flan ring,
keeping the pastry trimmings for the
lattice decoration.

3. Bake blind for 20 minutes (see note on
page 76).

4. For the mincemeat: grate the apple, skin
and all. Melt the butter and add it, with all
the other filling ingredients, to the apple.
Mix well.

5. Fill the flan with the mincemeat. Cut the
pastry trimmings into thin strips and lattice
the top of the flan with them, sticking
theends down with a little water. Brush the
lattice with water and sprinkle with caster
sugar. Return to the oven for 10-12
minutes, removing the flan ring after 5
minutes to allow the sides of the pastry to
cook to a pale brown.

FORTIFIED SWEET WHITE

Rhubarb Lattice Flan

SERVES 4-5

rich sweet shortcrust pastry made with
  170g/6oz flour (see page 86)
675g/1¹/₂lb rhubarb
30g/1oz caster sugar
caster sugar for sprinkling

For the glaze:
5ml/1 teaspoon arrowroot
15ml/1 tablespoon redcurrant jelly

1. Make the pastry and line a 20cm/8 inch flan ring, reserving the trimmings. Chill for 20 minutes.

2. Set the oven to 190°C/375°F/gas mark 5.

3. Prepare the rhubarb: cut it into 3cm/1¹/₂ inch lengths and stew very gently in 15ml/1 tablespoon water with the sugar until tender. Drain the fruit very well and reserve the juice.

4. Bake the pastry case blind for 20-25 minutes (see note on page 76).

5. Arrange the rhubarb neatly in the flan case.

6. Mix the arrowroot with enough of the fruit juice to make it smooth. Put the arrowroot mixture and the juice into a saucepan and bring it to the boil, stirring all the time. Add the jelly and boil for 30 seconds. Cool until warm, then pour into the flan, all over the fruit.

7. Roll out the pastry trimmings into long strips 5mm/¹/₄ inch wide. Twist the strips like barley sugar and arrange them in a lattice pattern over the flan, sticking the ends down with a little water. Brush each strip with water and sprinkle with caster sugar.

8. Return the flan to the oven until the pastry becomes a pale golden brown. Leave to cool on a wire rack.

SWEET WHITE

Pecan Pie

SERVES 8-10
For the pastry:
225g/8oz plain flour
pinch of salt
55g/2oz lard
85g/3oz butter
10ml/2 teaspoons sugar
30-45ml/2-3 tablespoons cold water

For the filling:
450g/1lb shelled pecan nuts
4 eggs
225g/8oz soft brown sugar
170g/6oz golden syrup
2.5ml/$^{1}/_{2}$ teaspoon salt
55g/2oz unsalted butter, melted
vanilla essence
30ml/2 tablespoons flour

1. Preheat the oven to 200°C/400°F/gas mark 6.

2. Sift the flour and salt into a bowl. Rub in the fats until the mixture resembles breadcrumbs.

3. Add the sugar and stir in enough water to bind the pastry together.

4. Roll out the pastry and use it to line a 28cm/11 inch flan case. Leave it in the refrigerator for about 30 minutes to relax. (This prevents shrinkage during cooking.)

5. Bake the pastry blind (see note on page 76).

6. Meanwhile, make the filling: chop half the pecan nuts. Whisk the eggs in a large bowl until frothy. Add the sugar, syrup, salt, melted butter and vanilla essence and beat well until thoroughly mixed. Stir in the sifted flour, making sure there are no lumps of flour in the mixture.

7. Scatter the chopped nuts over the cooked pastry case and pour over the filling. Arrange the remaining halved pecan nuts on top.

8. Bake on a baking sheet for 10 minutes and reduce to 170°C/325°F/gas mark 3 for 30-40 minutes or until the centre is just set. Serve warm or cold.

NOTE: The filling will separate slightly when it is cooked but this is normal and quite delicious.

FORTIFIED SWEET WHITE

Redcurrant and Blackcurrant Flan

SERVES 6
*sweet pastry made with 170g/6oz flour
  (see page 87)*

For the sponge lining:
2 eggs
55g/2oz caster sugar
55g/2oz flour, sifted

For the filling:
170g/6oz redcurrants, fresh or frozen
170g/6oz blackcurrants, fresh or frozen
85g/3oz caster sugar

For the glaze:
45ml/3 tablespoons redcurrant jelly

To serve:
whipped cream

1. Strip the redcurrants and blackcurrants off the stalks by holding each sprig of berries by the stalk in one hand and using a fork in the other to dislodge the berries. (If they are frozen, thaw and drain them.)

2. Put the black- and redcurrants in separate bowls and add half the sugar to each bowl, shaking to distribute the sugar without crushing the fruit. Leave for 4 hours. (Alternatively, simmer the fruits very gently with the sugar and a few spoons of water for 3 or 4 minutes to soften and cook them.) Make up the pastry and use it to line a deep 18cm/7 inch diameter flan ring. Refrigerate for 20 minutes.

3. Set the oven to 200°C/400°F/gas mark 6

4. Bake the flan case blind for 15 minutes (see note on page 76).

5. Make the sponge lining while the flan case is in the oven. Put the eggs and sugar into a bowl and set it over (not in) a pan of simmering water. Whisk steadily until the mixture is thick and mousse-like and the whisk will leave a ribbon-like trail when lifted. Remove from the heat and fold in the sifted flour. Remove the 'blind beans' from the half-cooked flan case. Pour the mixture in and return to the oven.

6. Bake for a further 10 minutes, then remove the flan ring and turn down the oven to 190°C/375°F/gas mark 5. Continue cooking until the pastry case is crisp and pale biscuit coloured, then remove and allow to cool.

7. Strain the fruit well (tipping both juices into a small saucepan) and arrange the black- and redcurrants in alternate quarters of the flan.

8. Add the redcurrant jelly to the juice and boil rapidly until syrupy and smooth. Cool until near setting, then spoon over the tart to give it a good clear glaze. Serve with whipped cream.

SWEET WHITE

Rhubarb Tart

SERVES 4-6
For the filling:
675g/1¹/₂lb trimmed rhubarb
15ml/1 tablespoon caster sugar

For the pastry:
225g/8oz flour
pinch of salt
55g/2oz butter
55g/2oz lard
5ml/1 teaspoon caster sugar

For the flan mixture:
2 eggs
125g/4¹/₂oz caster sugar
150ml/¹/₄ pint crème fraîche or single cream

1. Cut the rhubarb into 2.5cm/1 inch lengths and sprinkle with the sugar.

2. Set the oven to 190°C/375°F/gas mark 5.

3. Sift the flour into a medium-sized bowl with a pinch of salt. Rub the butter and lard into the flour until the mixture looks like breadcrumbs. Stir in the sugar. Add enough cold water to bind the pastry together.

4. Roll out the pastry and use it to line a 24cm/9 inch flan ring. Refrigerate it for 30 minutes.

5. Place the rhubarb and sugar in a shallow pan and cook over a gentle heat until the rhubarb softens slightly but still holds its shape. Allow to cool.

6. Bake the pastry blind (see note on page 76) in preheated oven for 10-15 minutes. Allow to cool. Turn the oven down to 150°C/300°F/ gas mark 2.

7. Mix the flan mixture ingredients together with a wooden spoon.

8. Arrange the rhubarb, without its juice, carefully in the baked flan case. Pour over the flan mixture and cook in the oven for 20-30 minutes. This tart is best served cold but not refrigerated.

SWEET WHITE

Charlotte's Higgledy Piggledy Tart

SERVES 6
walnut pastry made with 225g/8oz flour (see page 92)
150ml/¹/4 pint double cream, lightly whipped
290ml/¹/2 pint crème pâtissière (see page 152)
soft seasonal fruit such as apricots, oranges, plums, kiwis, bananas and strawberries
apricot glaze

1. Line a flan ring with the pastry. Relax for 30 minutes.

2. Preheat the oven to 375°F/190°C/gas mark 5.

3. Bake the flan case blind for 20 minutes (see note on page 76). Leave to cool.

4. Fold the cream into the almost cold crème pâtissière and pile into the flan case. Spread flat.

5. Prepare the fruit as for a fruit salad and arrange in a higgledy piggledy fashion.

6. Brush or spoon some warm apricot glaze over the top.

SWEET WHITE

Apple Flan Ménagère

SERVES 4
rich sweet shortcrust pastry made with 110g/4oz flour (see page 86)

For the filling and topping:
675g/1¹/2lb medium-sized dessert apples
caster sugar
45ml/3 tablespoons warm apricot glaze

1. Set the oven to 190°C/375°F/gas mark 5.

2. Roll out the pastry and line a 15cm/ 6 inch flan ring. Chill again for 10 minutes.

3. Bake blind for 20 minutes (see note on page 76).

4. Peel, quarter and core the apples. Using a stainless steel knife, thinly slice them into the flan ring (the apples will shrink considerably during cooking, so make sure that the flan is well filled). When the flan is nearly full, arrange the apple slices very neatly in overlapping circles.

5. Dust well with caster sugar and bake in the oven for about 20 minutes.

6. Remove the metal flan ring and return to the oven for a further 7-8 minutes.

7. When the flan is cooked, brush with apricot glaze and slide on to a wire rack to cool.

SWEET WHITE

Martha Stewart's Fudge Tart

This tart is served with crème anglaise and orange sauce.

40g/5oz semi-sweet chocolate, finely chopped
170g/6oz unsalted butter, cut into small pieces
340g/12oz granulated sugar
95g/3¹/₂oz flour
6 eggs, lightly beaten
deep 20cm/8 inch pâte brisée (see page 86)
  tart case, baked and cooled

For the crème anglaise:
570ml/1 pint milk
1 vanilla pod
170g/6oz granulated sugar
6 egg yolks
10ml/2 teaspoons cornflour
30ml/2 tablespoons brandy

For the orange sauce:
170ml/6 fl oz freshly squeezed orange juice
30ml/2 tablespoons Grand Marnier
225g/8oz granulated sugar
15ml/1 tablespoon grated orange rind

1. To make the filling: melt the chocolate and butter together in a basin over simmering water. When melted, remove from the heat and stir well to mix. Set aside to cool. Meanwhile preheat the oven to 180°C/350°F/gas mark 4.

2. Mix together the sugar, flour and eggs in a mixing bowl and whisk until well blended. Stir in the chocolate-butter mixture. Pour the filling into the tart case and bake for approximately 50 minutes, until the filling is set. Remove to a wire rack and let it cool completely.

3. To make the crème anglaise: put the milk and vanilla pod in a saucepan. Bring up to the boil. Turn off the heat and leave to infuse for 6 minutes. Remove the vanilla pod. Using an electric mixer, beat the sugar and egg yolks together until thick and fluffy. Add the cornflour. Mixing on low speed, gradually add the infused milk. When thoroughly incorporated, transfer the mixture to a heavy saucepan. Cook over low heat, stirring constantly, until the sauce thickens to a light, creamy mixture. (Do not let the mixture boil, or the egg yolks will curdle.) Remove the mixture from the heat and whisk in the brandy. Strain the mixture through a fine sieve and cool. Refrigerate until ready to use.

4. To make the orange sauce: mix together the orange juice, Grand Marnier and sugar in a heavy saucepan and cook over low heat, stirring constantly, until thick and syrupy and reduced by half. Remove from the heat, stir in the grated orange rind and leave to cool.

5. To serve: place a slice of the tart on a plate and spoon some crème anglaise around it. Drizzle a small amount of orange sauce into the crème anglaise in swirls.

FORTIFIED SWEET WHITE

Walnut, Pear and Apple Tart

SERVES 10
For the pastry:
225g/8oz flour
pinch of salt
5ml/1 teaspoon ground cinnamon
140g/5oz butter
110g/4oz caster sugar
55g/2oz walnuts, finely chopped
1 egg, beaten

For the filling:
3 cooking apples
3 William or Comice pears
30g/1oz butter
200g/7oz caster sugar
10ml/2 teaspoons ground cinnamon
juice of 1 lemon
110g/4oz sultanas
3 eggs
150ml/¹/4 pint double cream
170g/6oz walnuts, chopped

1. First make the pastry: sift the flour with the salt and cinnamon. Rub in the butter until the mixture resembles breadcrumbs. Mix in the sugar, then the walnuts.

2. Add the beaten egg to the mixture and mix it into a firm dough. Then leave the pastry to relax in the refrigerator for 30 minutes.

3. Roll out the pastry and use it to line a deep loose-bottomed 30cm/12 inch flan ring. Leave it in the refrigerator for about 30 minutes to relax.

4. Heat the oven to 190°C/375°F/gas mark 5.

5. Bake the pastry blind (see note on page 76).

6. Meanwhile, make the filling: peel and core the apples and pears and cut into chunks.

7. Melt the butter in a large heavy saucepan and, when foaming, add the apples and pears. Scatter on 85g/3oz of the caster sugar, the cinnamon, lemon juice and sultanas.

8. Toss the fruit over a medium heat for about 5 minutes, then strain, reserving the juice.

9. Spoon the lightly cooked pears and apples into the cooked pastry case.

10. Mix together the eggs, the remaining caster sugar, double cream and strained juice. Pour this mixture over the fruit and scatter the chopped walnuts over the top.

11. Place the flan in the oven and bake for 50 minutes, or until the centre is firm. (Cover with wet greaseproof paper if the tart begins to look too dark.)

12. Serve warm or cold.

SWEET WHITE

Tarte Tatin

SERVES 6
For the pastry:
170g/6oz plain flour
55g/2oz ground rice
140g/5oz butter
55g/2oz caster sugar
1 egg, beaten

For the topping:
110g/4oz butter
110g/4oz granulated sugar
900g/2lb cooking apples
grated rind of 1 lemon

1. Set the oven to 190°C/375°F/gas mark 5.

2. To make the pastry: sift the flour and ground rice into a large bowl. Rub in the butter until the mixture looks like breadcrumbs. Stir in the sugar. Add the egg and bind the dough together. Chill while you prepare the top.

3. To make the topping: melt the butter in a 25cm/10 inch frying pan with a metal handle. Add the granulated sugar and take off the heat. Peel, core and thickly slice the apples. Arrange the apple slices over the melted butter and sugar in the base of the frying pan. Sprinkle on the grated lemon rind.

4. Place the frying pan over a high flame until the butter and sugar start to caramelize. It may take 6-7 minutes and you will be able to smell the change – it is essential that the apples get dark. Remove from the heat.

5. Roll the pastry into a circle 5mm/$1/4$ inch thick, to fit the top of the pan. Lay it on top of the apples and press down lightly. Bake in the oven for 25-30 minutes.

6. Allow to cool slightly, turn out on to a plate and serve warm.

NOTE: If you do not have a frying pan with a metal handle, cook the apples in an ordinary frying pan. Let the butter and sugar mixture become well caramelized and tip into an ovenproof dish. Cover with the pastry and then bake in the oven on a hot baking sheet.

SWEET WHITE

Upside-Down Apricot Tart

This recipe has been adapted from one in *The Josceline Dimbleby Collection* published by Sainsbury's.

SERVES 6
For the pastry:
170g/6oz plain flour, plus extra for rolling
85g/3oz caster sugar
a pinch of salt
85g/3oz butter
1 egg, whisked

For the filling:
340g/12oz dried apricots
55g/2oz butter
85g/3oz caster sugar

1. Soak the dried apricots in a bowl of water for 2 hours.

2. Make the pastry: sift the flour, caster sugar and salt into a bowl. Gently melt the butter in a saucepan and stir into the flour mixture with a wooden spoon. Then thoroughly mix in the whisked egg until the dough is smooth. Press the mixture together into a ball, cover with cling film and leave in the refrigerator for at least 1 hour.

3. To make the filling: drain the apricots and pat dry with absorbent paper. Smear the base and sides of a 25cm/10 inch flan dish or tin (not one with a loose base) with the butter. Sprinkle the caster sugar all over and arrange the apricots neatly in circles on top of the sugar, rounded side down.

4. Now take the pastry from the refrigerator and roll out on a floured surface to a little more than the size of the flan dish. (If the pastry breaks, just press it together again and don't worry if it looks messy as it won't show.) Press the edges of the pastry firmly down within the flan dish. Pierce 2 or 3 holes in the pastry.

5. Heat the oven to 200°C/400°F/gas mark 6. Cook the tart in the centre of the oven for 25 minutes. Then turn down the oven to 170°C/325°F/gas mark 3 and cook the tart for a further 30-35 minutes. Remove from the oven and cool slightly. Then turn out the tart upside down on to a serving plate and eat while warm.

SWEET WHITE

Poached Pear and Polenta Tart with Soft Cream

SERVES 8
425ml/³/4 pint red wine
55g/2oz sugar
6 whole cloves
3 strips of lemon zest
2.5ml/¹/2 teaspoon ground cinnamon
5 pears

For the pastry:
140g/5oz butter at room temperature
140g/5oz sugar
3 egg yolks
200g/7oz flour
85g/3oz polenta
2.5ml/¹/2 teaspoon salt
extra 15ml/1 tablespoon polenta

For the soft cream:
150ml/¹/4 pint double cream
pear poaching liquid (see recipe)
brandy to taste
few drops of vanilla essence

1. Bring the wine, sugar, cloves, lemon zest and cinnamon to the boil in a medium-sized saucepan and simmer until reduced by about a fifth.

2. Peel the pears and cut them in half. Remove the cores carefully with an apple corer. Slice them into 1cm/¹/2 inch pieces. Put the pear slices into the red-wine mixture and cook carefully over a low heat for approximately 40 minutes or until the pears are tender. Lift them out with a draining spoon and allow them to cool to room temperature.

3. Strain the red wine to remove the lemon zest and cloves. Put the syrup back on the heat, bring to the boil and reduce by half. Some of this will be used to flavour the cream. Set the oven to 200°C/400°F/gas mark 6.

4. To make the pastry: cream the butter and sugar together until well blended. Add the egg yolks one at a time, beating well between each addition. Sift the flour, polenta and salt together and mix into the creamed mixture. Beat until the dough comes together, then knead lightly on a floured surface, adding more flour if necessary, until the pastry is no longer sticky. Rest the pastry in the refrigerator for 20 minutes.

5. Cut the dough in half. Press one half of the dough on to the base and sides of a 22cm/9 inch flan ring. Sprinkle the base with the extra polenta. Spoon the drained pears into the pastry shell.

6. Roll out the remaining dough to 1cm/¹/2 inch thickness. Using a fluted biscuit cutter, cut out as many circles as possible from the dough. Place them on top of the pears, starting on the outside.

Overlap the shapes and continue to cover the top.

7. Bake the tart in the preheated oven for about 30 minutes, covering with greaseproof paper if necessary after 20 minutes.

8. To make the soft cream: whip the double cream until soft peaks are formed. Flavour with some of the poaching liquid, the cognac and the vanilla essence to taste. Serve with the warm tart.

SWEET WHITE

Danish Shortcake

SERVES 4
85g/3oz plain flour
pinch of salt
55g/2oz butter
30g/1oz caster sugar
30g/1oz ground hazelnuts, browned
225g/8oz strawberries

For the redcurrant glaze:
60ml/4 tablespoons redcurrant jelly
15ml/1 tablespoon lemon juice

1. Set the oven to 190°C/375°F/gas mark 5.

2. Sift the flour, with a pinch of salt, into a bowl. Rub in the butter until the mixture resembles breadcrumbs. Stir in the sugar and nuts. Knead together to form a stiff dough.

3. On a lightly greased baking sheet, roll or press the pastry into a cake-sized flat round. Put in the refrigerator to relax for 10-15 minutes.

4. Bake in the oven for 15-20 minutes until pale brown all over. Loosen and leave to cool and harden on the tray.

5. To make the glaze: melt the redcurrant jelly with the lemon juice, but do not allow it to boil. Keep warm.

6. Place the cooked shortcake on a serving dish, arrange the strawberries neatly over the top and brush thickly with the melted redcurrant glaze

SWEET WHITE

Normandy Apple Flan

SERVES 6

This recipe has been taken from *The Observer French Cookery School* by Anne Willan of La Varenne.

pâte brisée made with 200g/7oz flour (see page 86
100g/3¹/₂oz butter
1 egg yolk
3.5ml/³/₄ level teaspoon salt
30-45ml/2-3 tablespoons cold water
3-4 ripe dessert apples

For the frangipane:
100g/3¹/₂oz butter
100g/3¹/₂oz caster sugar
1 egg, beaten
1 egg yolk
10ml/2 teaspoons Calvados or Kirsch
100g/3¹/₂oz blanched almonds, ground
30ml/2 tablespoons flour

To finish:
150ml/¹/₄ pint apricot jam glaze (see page 153)

1. Make the pâte brisée and wrap and chill for at least 30 minutes.

2. Set the oven at 200°C/400°F/gas mark 6, and place a baking sheet in the oven to heat. Roll out the dough, line a 25cm/10 inch tart tin with it, prick lightly with a fork, flute the edges and chill again until firm.

3. To make the frangipane: cream the butter, gradually beat in the sugar and continue beating until the mixture is light and soft. Gradually add the egg and yolk, beating well after each addition. Add the Calvados and Kirsch, then stir in the ground almonds and the flour. Pour the frangipane into the chilled pastry, spreading it evenly.

4. Peel the apples, halve them and scoop out the cores. Cut them crosswise in very thin slices and arrange them on the frangipane to make the spokes of a wheel, keeping the slices of each half apple together. Press them down gently until they touch the pastry dough base.

5. Bake the pie on the hot baking sheet near the top of the heated oven for 10-15 minutes until the pastry dough is beginning to brown. Turn down the oven to 180°C/350°F/gas mark 4, and continue cooking for 30-35 minutes or until the apples are tender and the frangipane is set.

6. Transfer to a rack to cool. A short time before serving, brush the tart with melted apricot jam glaze and serve at room temperature.

NOTE: Normandy apple flan is best eaten the day it is baked, but it can also be frozen. Just before serving, reheat to lukewarm in a low oven.

SWEET WHITE

Millefeuilles

SERVES 4-6

rough puff pastry made with 225g/8oz flour
  (see page 90) or puff pastry (see page 91)
30ml/2 tablespoons strawberry jam
290ml/¹/₂ pint double cream, whipped
225g/8oz icing sugar, sifted

1. Set the oven to 220°C/425°F/gas mark 7.

2. On a floured board, roll the pastry into a large thin rectangle about 30 x 20cm/12 x 8 inches. Place on a wet baking sheet. Prick all over with a fork.

3. Leave to relax, covered, for 20 minutes. Bake until brown. Allow to cool.

4. Cut the pastry into 3 neat strips, each 10 x 20cm/4 x 8 inches. (Keep the trimmings for decoration.) Choose the piece of pastry with the smoothest base, and reserve. Spread a layer of jam on the 2 remaining strips and cover with cream. Place them on top of each other and cover with the third, reserved, piece of pastry, smooth-side uppermost. Press down gently but firmly.

5. Mix the icing sugar with boiling water until it is thick, smooth and creamy. Be careful not to add too much water. Coat the icing on top of the pastry and, while still warm, sprinkle crushed cooked pastry trimmings along the edges of the icing. Allow to cool before serving.

NOTE I: To 'feather' the icing, put 15ml/1 tablespoon of warmed, smooth liquid jam in a piping bag with a 'writing' nozzle. Pipe parallel lines of jam down the length of the newly iced millefeuilles, about 2cm/³/₄ inch apart. Before the icing or jam is set, drag the back of a knife across the lines of jam. This will pull the lines into points where the knife crosses them. Repeat this every 5cm/2 inches in the same direction, and then drag the back of the knife in the opposite direction between the drag-lines already made.

NOTE II: Millefeuilles are also delicious covered with fresh strawberries and glazed with redcurrant glaze (see page 153) instead of icing the top.

SWEET SPARKLING WHITE

Jalousie

SERVES 4
rough puff pastry made with 110g/4oz
  flour (see page 90)
225g/8oz fresh apple marmalade (see page 154)
30ml/2 tablespoons smooth apricot jam
milk
caster sugar

1. Set the oven to 230°C/450°F/gas mark 8.

2. Roll the pastry into 2 thin rectangles, one about 2.5cm/1 inch bigger all round than the other. The smaller one should measure around 13 x 20cm/5 x 8 inches, and the larger 18 x 25cm/7 x 10 inches. Leave to relax for 20 minutes.

3. Prick the smaller one all over and bake until crisp and brown. Then take it out and turn it over on the baking sheet. Allow to cool.

4. Melt the jam in a small pan, and brush over the top of the cooked pastry. Spread the apple marmalade all over the cooked piece of pastry, on top of the jam.

5. Lay the larger piece of pastry on the board, dust it lightly with flour and fold it, gently so that nothing sticks, in half lengthways. Using a sharp knife, cut through the folded side of the pastry, at right angles to the edge, in parallel lines, as though you were cutting between the teeth of a comb. Leave an uncut margin about 2.5cm/1 inch wide, all round the other edges, so that when you open up the pastry you will have a solid border.

6. Now lay the cut pastry on top of the pastry covered with jam and apple marmalade and tuck the edges underneath. Brush the top layer carefully all over with milk (this is a bit messy as the apple keeps coming up between the pastry crust). Sprinkle well with sugar.

7. Bake in the oven until well browned, about 20 minutes. Serve cold or warm.

NOTE: Jalousie literally means shutters, and these are what the pie looks like.

RICH SWEET WHITE

Individual Apple Tarts with Calvados Crème Anglaise

SERVES 4

puff pastry made with 225g/8oz flour (see page 91
4 dessert apples
caster sugar
egg glaze
apricot glaze (see page 153)

To serve:
15ml/1 tablespoon Calvados
290ml/¹/₂ pint crème anglaise (see page 152), chilled

1. Set the oven to 200°C/400°F/gas mark 6.

2. Roll out the pastry and cut into 4 circles 2mm/¹/₈ inch thick and 12.5cm/5 inches in diameter. Place on a damp baking sheet. With a sharp knife, trace an inner circle about 1cm/¹/₂ inch from the edge of the pastry. Do not cut all the way through the pastry.

3. Peel, core and slice the apples finely and arrange in concentric circles within the border of each pastry tart. Using a sharp knife, mark a pattern on the pastry border.

4. Sprinkle lightly with caster sugar. Brush the pastry rim with egg glaze, taking care not to let it drop down the sides of the pastry.

5. Flour the blade of a knife and use this to 'knock up' the sides of the pastry. Chill for 15 minutes.

6. Bake for 20 minutes. Leave to cool slightly and then brush liberally with warm apricot glaze.

7. Add the Calvados to the well-chilled crème anglaise. Serve the tarts warm with the cold custard.

SWEET WHITE

Gâteau Pithivier

SERVES 6

puff pastry made with 450g/1lb flour (see page 91)
1 egg beaten with 2. 5ml/1/2 teaspoon salt
110g/4oz apricot jam glaze (see page 153)

For the almond filling:
125g/4¹/2oz butter, softened
125g/4¹/2oz sugar
1 egg
1 egg yolk
125g/4¹/2oz whole blanched almonds, skinned and ground
15g/¹/2oz flour
30ml/2 tablespoons rum

1. Make the puff pastry and chill.

2. For the filling: cream the butter in a bowl, add the sugar and beat thoroughly. Beat in the egg and the yolk; then stir in the almonds, flour and rum.

3. Roll out half the puff pastry to a circle, about 27cm/11 inches in diameter. Using a pan lid as a guide, cut out a 25cm/10 inch circle from this with a sharp knife, angling the knife slightly. Roll out the remaining dough slightly thicker than for the first round and cut out another 25cm/10 inch circle. Set the thinner circle on a baking sheet, mound the filling in the centre, leaving a 2.5cm/1 inch border, and brush the border with egg glaze. Set the second circle on top and press the edges together firmly.

4. Scallop the edge of the gâteau by pulling it in at intervals with the back of a knife. Brush the gâteau with egg glaze and, working from the centre, score the top in curves like the petals of a flower. Do not cut through to the filling. Chill the gâteau for 15-20 minutes. Set the oven to 220°C/425°F/gas mark 7.

5. Bake the gâteau in the heated oven for 30-35 minutes or until it is firm, puffed and brown. Brush the gâteau while still hot with melted apricot glaze. Transfer to a rack to cool.

SWEET SPARKLING WHITE

Chocolate Profiteroles

MAKES 30
For the profiteroles:
3-egg quantity choux pastry (see page 95)

For the filling and topping:
570ml/1 pint whipped cream, sweetened with
  15ml/1 tablespoon icing sugar
110g/4oz chocolate, chopped
15g/¹/₂oz butter

1. Set the oven to 200°C/400°F/gas mark 6.

2. Put teaspoons of the choux mixture on a wet baking sheet, about 8cm/3 inches apart.

3. Bake for 20-30 minutes. The profiteroles should swell, and become fairly brown. If they are taken out when only slightly brown, they will be soggy when cool.

4. Make a hole the size of a pea in the base of each profiterole and return to the oven for 5 minutes to allow the insides to dry out. Cool on a wire rack.

5. When cold fill each profiterole with the sweetened cream, using a forcing bag fitted with a small plain nozzle.

6. Put the chocolate into a bowl with the butter and melt over a pan of simmering water.

7. Dip the tops of the profiteroles in the chocolate and allow to cool.

NOTE: If no piping bag is available for filling the profiteroles, they can be split, allowed to dry out, and filled with cream or crème pâtissière when cold, and the icing can be spooned over the top. However, made this way they are messier to eat in the fingers.

FORTIFIED SWEET WHITE

Coffee Eclairs

MAKES 20-25
3-egg quantity choux pastry (see
  page 95)

For the filling and topping:
425ml/³/4 pint double cream, lightly whipped
  and sweetened with 15ml/1 tablespoon icing
  sugar, or crème pâtissière (see page 152)
225g/8oz icing sugar
30ml/2 tablespoons very strong hot black coffee

1. Heat the oven to 200°C/400°F/gas mark
6. Wet 2 baking sheets. Make up the choux
pastry.

2. Using a forcing bag with a 1cm/¹/2 inch
plain nozzle, pipe 5cm/2 inch lengths of
choux pastry on to the baking sheets (keep
them well separated as choux pastry swells
during cooking). Bake for 25-30 minutes
until crisp and pale brown.

3. Make a pea-sized hole in each one with a
skewer to allow the steam to escape and
return to the oven for 5 minutes to dry the
insides out. Then place on a wire rack to
cool.

4. Put the sweetened cream (or the crème
pâtissière) into a forcing bag fitted with a
medium nozzle. Pipe the cream into the
éclairs through the hole made by the
skewer, until well filled.

5. Mix the icing sugar and very hot coffee
together and beat with a wooden spoon
until smooth. The mixture should be just
runny.

6. Dip each éclair upside down into the
icing so that the top becomes neatly
coated.

7. Set aside to dry. Alternatively, the icing
can be carefully spooned along the top
ridge of each éclair.

NOTE: The éclairs may be split lengthways
when cooked, allowed to dry out, and
filled with cream or crème pâtissière when
cold. The tops are then replaced and the
icing spooned over but they are then
messier to eat in the fingers.

FORTIFIED SWEET WHITE

Gâteau St Honoré

SERVES 6

pâte sucrée made with 110g/4oz flour (see
  page 95)
3-egg quantity choux pastry (see page 95)
570ml/1 pint crème pâtissière (see page 152)
  double quantity)
110g/4oz granulated sugar

1. Line an 18cm/7 inch flan ring with the
pâte sucrée and bake it blind at
190°C/375°F/gas mark 5 (see note on page
76) for 20 minutes until biscuit coloured.

2. Make the profiteroles: increase the oven
temperature to 200°C/400°F/gas mark 6.
Wet 2 baking sheets.

3. Put teaspoonfuls of the choux mixture
on to the baking sheets and bake for 25
minutes until hard and pale brown.

4. Make a pea-sized hole in the base of
each choux bun with a skewer and return
to the oven for 5 minutes to dry the insides
out. Place on a wire rack to cool.

5. Using a forcing bag fitted with a plain
nozzle, pipe the crème pâtissière into 17
even-sized profiteroles, piping the mixture
through the previously made holes.
Spread the remaining crème pâtissière into
the bottom of the empty flan case. Pile the
profiteroles into a pyramid on top of the
filling.

6. Slowly heat the sugar in a heavy
saucepan until it caramelizes to a pale
liquid toffee.

7. Pour the caramel over the profiteroles.

NOTE: Vast pyramids of profiteroles filled
as here, or with whipped cream, form the
traditional French wedding cake or croque
en bouche. Sometimes icing sugar is sifted
over the whole creation.

SWEET SPARKLING WHITE

Apricot Ring

SERVES 6
110g/4oz apricots
150ml/¹/₄ pint sugar syrup (see page 153)
3-egg quantity choux pastry (see page 95)
30ml/2 tablespoons apricot jam
140g/5oz icing sugar
290ml/¹/₂ pint double cream, whipped
30g/1oz almonds, browned

1. Set the oven to 200°C/400°F/gas mark 6.

2. Wash and halve the apricots and remove the stones. Poach in the sugar syrup until just tender (about 15 minutes). Drain well and leave to cool.

3. Pipe the choux paste mixture into a circle about 15cm/6 inches in diameter on a wet baking tray. Cook for about 30 minutes until brown and crisp.

4. Split horizontally with a bread knife. Scoop out any uncooked paste and discard; leave on a wire rack to cool. Heat the jam and spread it on the base of the choux ring.

5. Mix 30g/1oz of the icing sugar with the whipped cream and fold in the apricots. Then spoon the mixture on to the base and press the lid on firmly.

6. Mix the rest of the icing sugar with a little boiling water until just runny. Coat the top of the choux ring with the icing and, while still wet, sprinkle with browned almonds.

SWEET WHITE

Feuilleté de Poires Tiède

SERVES 4
2 William pears
290ml/¹/₂ pint sugar syrup (see page 153)
puff pastry made with 340g/12oz flour (see page 91)
290ml/¹/₂ pint double cream, lightly whipped
290ml/¹/₂ pint crème anglaise (see page 152)
55ml/2 fl oz Poire William liqueur
icing sugar

1. Peel the pears, cut in quarters and remove the cores. Poach carefully in the sugar syrup until they are soft.

2. Set the oven to 220°C/425°F/gas mark 7.

3. On a lightly floured board, roll the pastry into 4 neat rectangles 10 x 6cm/ 4 x 2¹/₂ inches. Relax in the refrigerator for 20 minutes.

4. Bake until brown for 15 minutes. Cut in half horizontally, remove any uncooked dough and return to the turned-off oven to dry out. Remove from the oven.

5. Fold the lightly whipped cream into the crème anglaise. Flavour with the liqueur.

6. Sandwich the pastry slices together with the cream mixture and slices of warm poached pear. Dust the pastry lightly with icing sugar.

SWEET WHITE

Apple Strudel

SERVES 6

strudel pastry made with 285g/10oz flour (see
*   page 94) rolled to at least 40 x 60cm/15 x 24*
*   inches*

For the filling:
900g/2lb cooking apples
handful of currants, sultanas and raisins
30g/1oz brown sugar
2.5ml/¹/2 teaspoon cinnamon
pinch of ground cloves
45ml/3 tablespoons crumbs, browned
grated rind and juice of ¹/2 lemon
85g/3oz melted butter
icing sugar

1. Heat the oven to 200°C/400°F/gas
mark 6. Grease a baking sheet.

2. Prepare the filling: peel, core and slice
the apples in such a way that they don't
have very sharp corners which will pierce
the delicate pastry, and mix together with
the dried fruit, sugar, spices, crumbs,
lemon rind and juice.

3. Flour a large tea towel. Lay the pastry on
this. If you have not got a big enough piece
of pastry, several smaller ones will do, but
they must be overlapped well.

4. Brush with butter. Spread the filling over
the pastry evenly. Using the tea towel to
help, roll up as for a Swiss roll, trying to
maintain a fairly close roll. Lift the cloth
and gently tip the strudel on to the baking
sheet. Brush with melted butter.

5. Bake in the oven until a golden brown
(about 40 minutes). Dust with icing sugar
while still warm.

NOTE: In delicatessens, strudels are
generally sold in one-portion sizes.
To make these you need leaves of pastry
about 22cm/9 inches square. As they are
easier to handle, they can be lifted without
the aid of the cloth – just flour the table top
to prevent sticking. Bake for 20 minutes.

SWEET WHITE

Baklava

Claudia Roden's book *A New Book of Middle Eastern Food* is fascinating to read and an excellent book from which to cook. At Leith's she is one of our very special guest lecturers. The students love to see her make both this baklava and the konafa.

170g/6oz unsalted butter, melted
450g/1lb filo pastry (24 sheets)
340g/12oz pistachios, walnuts or almonds,
  ground or finely chopped

For the syrup:
450g/1lb sugar
290ml/¹/₂ pint water
30ml/2 tablespoons lemon juice
30ml/2 tablespoons orange blossom water

1. First make the syrup: put the sugar, water and lemon juice into a saucepan, dissolve over a gentle heat and then simmer until thick enough to coat the back of a wooden spoon. Add the orange blossom water and simmer for a further 2 minutes. Leave to cool and then refrigerate.

2. Preheat the oven to 160°C/325°F/gas mark 3.

3. Brush melted butter on the base and sides of a deep baking sheet. Put half the filo sheets into the roasting pan, brushing each sheet with melted butter and overlapping or folding the sides over where necessary.

4. Spread the nuts evenly over the pastry, spoon over 60ml/4 tablespoons of the

sugar syrup and then cover with the remaining sheets of filo, brushing each one as you layer it up. Brush the top layer with butter. Cut diagonally into lozenge shapes with a sharp, serrated knife.

5. Bake for 45 minutes, increase the oven temperature to 220°C/425°F/gas mark 7 and bake for a further 15 minutes or until well risen and golden brown.

6. Remove from the oven and pour the chilled syrup over the hot baklava. Leave to cool.

7. When cold, cut into lozenge shapes as before and place on a serving dish.

RICH SWEET WHITE/SPARKLING

Konafa

450g/1lb konafa pastry, available in
*   delicatessens*
225g/8oz unsalted butter, melted

For the syrup:
450g/1lb sugar
290ml/¹/2 pint water
30ml/2 tablespoons lemon juice
30ml/2 tablespoons orange flower water

For the filling:
90ml/6 tablespoons ground rice
60ml/4 tablespoons sugar
1 litre/1³/4 pints milk
150ml/¹/4 pint double cream

1. First make the syrup: put the sugar, water and lemon juice into a saucepan, dissolve over a gentle heat and then simmer until thick enough to coat the back of a wooden spoon. Add the orange blossom water and simmer for a further 2 minutes. Leave to cool and then refrigerate.

2. Mix the ground rice and sugar to a smooth paste with 150ml/¹/4 pint of the milk. Bring the rest of the milk up to the boil and gradually add the ground rice paste slowly, stirring vigorously. Simmer, stirring to prevent it catching on the bottom, until very thick. Allow to cool, add the cream and mix well.

3. Preheat the oven to 160°C/325°F/gas mark 3.

4. Put the konafa pastry into a large bowl. Pull out and separate the strands as much as possible with your fingers so that they do not stick together too much. Pour in the melted butter and work it in very well. Put half the pastry in a large, deep ovenproof dish. Spread the filling evenly over and cover with the remaining pastry. Flatten it with the palm of your hand.

5. Bake for 1 hour, increase the oven temperature to 220°C/425°F/gas mark 7 and bake for a further 10-15 minutes or until golden brown.

6. Remove from the oven and pour the cold syrup over the hot konafa.

NOTE: Konafa can be made with a variety of fillings, such as cheese, nuts and cinnamon or sliced bananas. They can also be made as individually rolled pastries instead of one large pastry.

RICH SWEET WHITE/SPARKLING

Almond Pastry Fruit Flan

SERVES 6
almond pastry made with 110g/4oz flour (see page 96)

For the glaze:
45ml/3 tablespoons apricot jam
squeeze of lemon juice
15ml/1 tablespoon water

a selection of: oranges, pears, grapes, cherries, strawberries, bananas, apples, plums, etc., depending on the season

1. Set the oven to 200°C/400°F/gas mark 6.

2. On a baking sheet roll or press the pastry into a 20cm/8 inch circle. Decorate the edges with a fork or the point of a sharp knife (pressed broad side into the pastry) or by pinching between fingers and thumb. Prick lightly all over.

3. Bake for about 15 minutes until a pale biscuit colour. Loosen with a palette knife and allow to cool slightly and harden on the baking sheet. Slip on to a wire rack to cool completely.

4. Meanwhile, prepare the apricot glaze: melt the jam with the lemon juice and water. Boil up, sieve and keep warm until ready for use. Do not stir too much or the glaze will be bubbly.

5. Prepare the fruits as you would for a fruit salad, but leaving any that discolour (such as apples or pears) until you assemble the flan.

6. Brush the pastry with some of the apricot glaze (this helps to stick the fruit in place and prevents the pastry from becoming too soggy).

7. Arrange the fruit in neat overlapping circles, taking care to get contrasting colours next to each other. Brush with apricot glaze as you go, especially on apples, pears or bananas. When all the fruit is in place, brush with the rest of the glaze.

NOTE: This flan should not be put together too far in advance as the pastry will become soggy in about 2 hours.

SWEET WHITE

Candied Lemon Tart

SERVES 6

pâte sucrée made with 170g/6oz flour (see page 95)
4 eggs
1 egg yolk
200g/7oz caster sugar
150ml/1/4 pint double cream
juice and grated rind of 2 lemons
icing sugar

To glaze:
1 lemon
150ml/1/4 pint sugar syrup (see page 153)

1. Set the oven to 170°C/325°F/gas mark 3.

2. Line a 18cm/7 inch flan ring with pâte sucrée. Relax for 30 minutes and then bake blind for 15 minutes (see note on page 76). Leave to cool on a wire rack. Reduce the oven to 150°C/300°F/gas mark 2.

3. For the filling: mix the eggs and extra yolk with the sugar and beat lightly with a whisk until smooth. Add the cream and whisk again. Add the lemon juice and rind. It will thicken alarmingly but do not worry.

4. Put the pastry case back on to a baking sheet and spoon in the lemon filling. Bake for 50 minutes; if it becomes too brown, cover the top with a piece of tin foil.

5. While the pie is cooking, prepare the glazed lemon rind. With a potato peeler, pare the rind from the lemon very finely, making sure that there is no pith on the back of the strips. Cut into very fine shreds.

6. Simmer these shreds in the sugar syrup until tender, glassy and candied. Leave to cool on greaseproof paper.

7. When the tart is cooked, remove the flan ring and leave to cool.

8. When cool, dust thickly and evenly with sifted icing sugar and arrange the candied shreds on top.

SWEET WHITE

Rum Baba

SERVES 4
For the sugar syrup:
170g/6oz loaf sugar
225ml/8 fl oz water
30ml/2 tablespoons rum

For the yeast mixture:
110g/4oz plain flour
15g/¹/₂oz fresh yeast
15g/¹/₂oz caster sugar
90ml/6 tablespoons warm milk
2 egg yolks
grated rind of ¹/₂ lemon
55g/2oz butter

For the decoration (optional):
fresh fruit such as grapes and raspberries
150ml/¹/₄ pint double or whipping cream,
  lightly whipped

1. First make the sugar syrup: dissolve the sugar in the water and boil rapidly for 3 minutes. The syrup should be boiled to the 'thread' (when a little syrup is put between finger and thumb and the fingers are opened, the syrup should form a short thread). Add the rum.

2. Now make the yeast mixture: sift the flour into a warmed bowl. Mix the yeast with 2.5ml/¹/₂ teaspoon of the sugar, 5ml/1 teaspoon of the flour and enough milk to make a batter-like consistency.

3. Whisk the egg yolks, remaining sugar and lemon rind until fluffy. Clarify the butter: melt it slowly in a saucepan, see that it separates and strain through a clean

'J' cloth or muslin, leaving the sediment behind. Make a well in the centre of the flour and add the yeast and beaten eggs. With your fingers, mix together and gradually draw in the flour from the sides, adding more milk as you take in more flour. When all the flour has been incorporated, beat with your hand until soft and smooth.

4. Gradually add the clarified butter, kneading and slapping the dough until it looks like a very thick batter and no longer sticks to the palm of your hand. Cover and leave to rise in a warm place (e.g. the airing cupboard) for about 45 minutes. It should double in size.

5. Set the oven to 190°C/375°F/gas mark 5. Grease a 1 litre/1¹/₂ pint savarin (ring) mould with plenty of butter.

6. When the dough has risen, beat it down again and use to fill the mould. It should half-fill the tin. Cover and leave to prove (rise again) for 10-15 minutes in a warm place. Then bake in the oven for 30-35 minutes until golden brown.

7. Turn out on to a wire rack and, while still warm, prick with a toothpick and brush with plenty of rum syrup until the baba is really soaked and shiny. Put on a serving dish. Serve plain or surround with fresh fruit and pile the whipped cream in the centre.

NOTE: If using dried or easy-blend yeast see note on page 12-13.

Strawberry Tartlets

MAKES 20
pâte sucrée made with 170g/6oz flour (see page 95)

For the filling:
225g/8oz petit Suisse cheese
55g/2oz caster sugar
450g/1lb strawberries, hulled
60ml/4 tablespoons redcurrant jelly, melted

1. Set the oven to 190°C/375°F/gas mark 5.

2. Roll out the pastry thinly and use it to line tartlet tins. Bake blind for about 15 minutes or until a pale biscuit colour (see note on page 76). Remove the papers and the 'blind' beans. If the pastry is not quite cooked, return to the oven for 5 minutes. Carefully take out the pastry cases and leave to cool on a wire rack.

3. Cream the cheese with the caster sugar and place a teaspoonful of this mixture at the bottom of each case. Arrange the strawberries, cut in half if necessary, on top of the cheese and brush lightly with warm melted redcurrant jelly.

SWEET WHITE

Sablé aux Fraises

This recipe has been adapted from *The Roux Brothers on Pâtisserie.*

SERVES 6
pâte sablée made with 280g/10oz flour (see page 87)
675g/1¹/₂lb strawberries, hulled and sliced
425ml/³/₄ pint raspberry coulis (see page 153)
55g/2oz icing sugar

1. Set the oven to 200°C/400°F/gas mark 6.

2. Divide the dough into 2 pieces to make for easier rolling.

3. Roll out the doughs very thinly and cut into a total of 18 x 10cm/4 inch circles. Bake in the preheated oven for 8 minutes or until a pale golden. Lift on to a wire rack and leave to cool.

4. Cut the strawberries in half and mix them with two-thirds of the raspberry coulis. Leave to macerate.

5. Place a pastry base on 6 pudding plates. Arrange a few macerated strawberries on top. Cover with a second pastry base and more strawberries. Cover with a third piece of pastry and sprinkle generously with icing sugar.

6. Serve the coulis separately or poured around the sablés.

NOTE: Do not assemble this pudding in advance as the pastry will become soggy.

Savarin aux Fruits

In the absence of a savarin mould, use an ordinary cake tin. The fruit should then be piled on top of the cake.

SERVES 4

For the savarin:
110g/4oz plain flour
7g/¹/4oz fresh yeast
15g/¹/2oz caster sugar
2 egg yolks
grated rind of ¹/2 lemon
90ml/6 tablespoons lukewarm milk
55g/2oz butter, softened

For the syrup:
170g/6oz loaf sugar
225ml/8 fl oz water
2 drops vanilla essence

For the fruit mixture:
675-900g/1¹/2-2lb in total of bananas, cherries, plums, grapes, oranges, apricots, apples and pineapple

To serve:
290ml/¹/2 pint crème Chantilly (see page 152)

1. Sift the flour into a warmed bowl. Mix the yeast with 2. 5ml/¹/2 teaspoon of the sugar, add 15ml/1 teaspoon flour and enough milk (about 60ml/4 tablespoons) to give a batter-like consistency.

2. Whisk the egg yolks, remaining sugar and lemon rind until fluffy.

3. Make a well in the centre of the flour and add the yeast and egg mixtures. Mix them together with the fingers of one hand, and then gradually draw in the flour from the sides, adding milk as you take in more flour. When all the flour has been incorporated, beat with your hand until very soft and smooth.

4. Gradually add the butter, kneading and slapping the dough until it looks like a thick batter, and no longer sticks to the palm of your hand.

5. Cover and leave to rise in a warm place for about 45 minutes. It should double in size.

6. Dissolve the sugar in the water and boil rapidly for 2 minutes, or until syrupy. When cool, add the vanilla essence.

7. Prepare the fruit as for a fruit salad and moisten with 1-2 spoons of the syrup.

8. Heat the oven to 190°C/375°F/gas mark 5. Butter a savarin or large ring mould thickly. When the dough has risen, beat it down again and fill the savarin mould. It should half-fill the tin. Cover and leave to prove (rise again) for 10-15 minutes in a warm place.

9. Bake in the oven for 30-35 minutes until golden brown. Turn out on to a wire rack and, while still hot, prick all over with a toothpick and brush with plenty of warm sugar syrup.

10. Allow to cool. Put on a serving dish and

again brush with syrup until the cake is completely soaked. Fill the centre with the fruit. Serve with crème Chantilly.

NOTE: If using dried yeast, use half the amount called for, mix it with 45ml/3 tablespoons of the liquid (warmed to blood temperature) and 5ml/1 teaspoon sugar. Leave until frothy, about 15 minutes, then proceed. If the yeast does not go frothy, it is dead and unusable. If using easy-blend yeast, use half the quantity called for and add it to the dry ingredients.

Meringues (Swiss Meringues)

This quantity makes 50 miniature or 12 large meringues.

4 egg whites
pinch of salt
225g/8oz caster sugar

For the filling:
whipped cream

1. Set the oven to 110°C/225°F/gas mark ½. Place silicone paper on 2 baking sheets.

2. Whisk the egg whites with a pinch of salt until stiff but not dry. Add 30ml/2 tablespoons of the sugar and whisk again until very stiff and shiny. Then fold in the rest of the sugar.

3 Drop the meringue mixture on to the paper-covered baking sheets in spoonfuls set fairly far apart. Use a teaspoon for tiny meringues; a dessertspoon for larger ones.

4. Bake in the oven for about 2 hours until the meringues are dry right through and will lift easily off the paper. When cold, sandwich the meringues together in pairs with whipped cream.

NOTE : If making a meringue mixture with a powerful electric mixer, when the whites are stiff gradually add half the sugar. Whisk again until very shiny, then add the remaining sugar and whisk lightly until just incorporated.

Italian Meringue

This meringue is much more laborious to make than Swiss meringue, but it has the advantage that once mixed it is extremely stable. Provided it is covered with polythene or a damp cloth to prevent drying out, the cook can leave it for hours before using it without risk of disintegration and, as it hardly swells at all in the oven, it is ideal for piped meringue baskets, vacherins, etc.

It cooks rather faster than Swiss meringue (see page 141), is chalkier and more powdery, and stays a brilliant white. Although it is not as nice to eat as Swiss meringue, it is useful if catering for large numbers, and delicious if filled with strawberries and cream.

225g/8oz lump sugar
90ml/6 tablespoons water
4 egg whites

1. Put the sugar and water in a heavy saucepan.

2. Without stirring, bring it slowly to the boil. If any sugar crystals get stuck to the side of the pan, brush them down into the syrup with a clean wet brush. Use a sugar thermometer if available.

3. The syrup is ready when it reaches 116°C/240°F. Alternatively, test for the 'soft ball' stage (see note).

4. While the syrup is gently boiling to the correct stage, whisk the egg whites to stiff peaks.

5. If the whites are in an electric mixer, pour the bubbling hot syrup on to them in a steady stream while whisking, taking care not to pour the syrup on to the wires of the whisk – it cools fast against the cold metal and can harden and stick to the whisk. If whisking the whites by hand, and in the absence of anyone to pour as you whisk, pour the syrup on to the whites in stages, about one-third at a time, whisking hard between each addition and working as fast as possible. The syrup must be bubbling hot as it hits the egg white to partially cook it.

6. Once the syrup is all in, whisk hard until the mixture is stiff and shiny and absolutely stable. If the whisk is lifted, the meringue should not flow at all.

7. Keep covered with polythene or a damp cloth if not using at once.

NOTE: To test the syrup, drop a teaspoonful into a cup of cold water. If the syrup has reached the right temperature, it will set into a soft ball which can be squashed between the fingers. If the syrup forms a hard ball, like a hard-boiled sweet, it has reached too high a temperature to make Italian meringue.

Almond Dacquoise with Apricot Purée

SERVES 6
5 egg whites
pinch of salt
large pinch cream of tartar
285g/10oz caster sugar
110g/4oz ground almonds
290ml/¹/₂ pint double cream

For the purée:
225g/8oz fresh apricots, halved and stoned
sugar to taste

1. Preheat the oven to 140°C/275°F/gas mark 1.

2. Line 2 baking sheets with bakewell paper and mark a 22.5cm/9 inch diameter circle on each.

3. Whisk the egg whites, with a pinch of salt and the cream of tartar, until stiff, then add 40ml/2¹/₂ tablespoons of the sugar. Whisk again until very stiff and shiny.

4. Fold in the rest of the sugar. Fold in the ground almonds.

5. Divide the mixture between the 2 baking sheets and spread the meringue to the correct size.

6. Bake for 1 hour. Cool slightly, remove from the bakewell paper and leave to become completely cold.

7. While the meringues are baking, make the apricot purée. Put the apricots into a saucepan with 30ml/2 tablespoons sugar and enough water to come halfway up the apricots. Cook slowly, stirring occasionally, until the apricots are tender.

8. Process the poached apricots with enough of the liquid to make a thick purée. Taste and add extra sugar if required. Cool.

9. Whip the cream. Sandwich the cake together with half the cream mixed with the apricot purée. Decorate the top of the dacquoise with rosettes of cream.

NOTE: When making a meringue mixture with a powerful electric mixer, add half the sugar when the whites are stiff. Whisk again until very shiny and then add the remaining sugar and whisk lightly until just incorporated.

SWEET WHITE

Meringue Cuite

'Cooked' meringue is a professional chef's meringue used largely for frosting petits fours, for fruit pie tops and as unbaked frosting for cakes. It is only worth making if an electric whisk is handy, when it is easy. It produces an even chalkier and finer-textured meringue than Italian meringue and, if used on baked confections, comes out of the oven shiny, smooth and pale-biscuit coloured.

Like Italian meringue, meringue cuite is very stable in the oven, hardly swelling at all and unlikely to cook out of shape. For this reason it is often used for intricate work such as the meringue basket on page 145. When baked at very low temperatures, it emerges smooth and shiny-white.

The proportions of egg white to sugar are the same as for most meringues, but the sugar used is confectioner's (icing) sugar, rather than caster. Sometimes a 50-50 mixture of caster and icing sugar is used and occasionally, when the meringue is for a fine cake frosting that will not be baked, the sugar content can be increased above the normal 55g/2oz per small egg white to 85g/3oz.

4 egg whites
225g/8oz icing sugar
3 drops vanilla essence

1. Use a whisking bowl that will fit snugly on a saucepan of simmering water, without the bottom of the bowl being in direct contact with the water. Whisk the whites until stiff and set them over the water.

2. Add the sifted icing sugar. It flies about in sugar-dust clouds so take care. Whisk until thick and absolutely stable – there should be no movement at all when the whisk is lifted. Add the vanilla essence.

3. Keep covered with polythene or a damp cloth if not using at once.

NOTE: If the mixture is whisked in a strong machine, a good result can be achieved without beating over heat. But it takes a good 15 minutes to get a perfect 'cuite' consistency.

Strawberry Meringue Basket

This is a classic meringue cuite recipe. In order to make this 18cm/7 inch diameter basket, you will need to make the meringue in 2 batches – it is too great a quantity to be managed at once.

SERVES 8
For the meringue cuite:
8 egg whites
450g/1lb icing sugar
6 drops vanilla flavouring

For the filling:
450g/1lb fresh strawberries, hulled
425ml/³/4 pint double cream, whipped

1. Set the oven to 140°C/275°F/gas mark 1. Line 2 large baking sheets with silicone 'bakewell' paper. Draw 2 x 18cm/7 inch diameter circles on each piece of paper and turn over.

2. Make up the first batch of meringue cuite. Put half the egg whites with half the sifted sugar into a mixing bowl and set over, not in, a pan of simmering water. Whisk, with a large hand balloon whisk or electric hand whisk, until the meringue is thick and will hold its shape. This may well take up to 10 minutes of vigorous beating. (A very good imitation meringue cuite can be made by whisking the egg whites and sugar together in a powerful mixer without bothering to heat the meringue. However, hand whisks tend to overheat in the time it takes to achieve the correct solidity of meringue if not beaten over heat.)

3. Add half of the vanilla flavouring. Remove the bowl and whisk for a further 2 minutes.

4. Remove the meringue from the heat and put into a forcing bag fitted with a 1cm/¹/2 inch plain nozzle. Squeeze gently to get rid of any pockets of air. Hold the bag upright in your right hand and, using your left hand to guide the nozzle, pipe a circular base on the first baking sheet, on one of your pencilled circles. Pipe 3 x 18cm/7 inch empty rings on the 3 remaining pencilled circles.

5. Bake for 45-60 minutes until dry and crisp. Cool on a wire rack.

6. Make up the second batch of meringue cuite using the remaining ingredients. Return the round of cooked meringue to the baking sheet. Use a little uncooked mixture to fix the hoops on the round, one on top of the other.

7. Put the remaining mixture into a forcing bag fitted with a rose nozzle. Cover the hoops with the meringue. Then bake at the same temperature for 45-60 minutes until set and crisp. Cool.

8. Fill with the lightly whipped cream and strawberries just before serving.

LIGHT SWEET WHITE

Walnut and Lemon Meringue Cake

SERVES 6

4 egg whites
pinch of salt
225g/8oz caster sugar
140g/5oz walnuts
290ml/¹/₂ pint double cream
60ml/4 tablespoons lemon curd (see page 153)

1. Set the oven to 190°C/375°F/gas mark 5.

2. Line 2 x 20cm/8 inch cake tins with lightly oiled tin foil or simply line the base with silicone paper and oil the sides of the tin.

3. Whisk the egg whites with a pinch of salt until stiff, then add 30ml/2 table-spoons of the sugar. Whisk again until very stiff and shiny.

4. Fold in the rest of the sugar.

5. Chop the nuts roughly, reserving a handful, and stir into the mixture.

6. Divide the mixture between the 2 tins, smoothing the tops slightly.

7. Bake the cakes for 40 minutes. Turn them out on a wire rack and peel off the paper.

8. Whip the cream and mix half of it with the lemon curd. Sandwich the cakes with this.

9. Use the rest of the whipped cream and nuts for the top.

NOTE: When making a meringue mixture with a powerful electric mixer, when the whites are stiff add half the sugar gradually. Whisk again until very shiny and then add the remaining sugar and whisk lightly until just incorporated.

SWEET WHITE

Meringue Baskets

MAKES 6
2 egg whites
pinch of salt
110g/4oz caster sugar

For the filling:
double cream, lightly whipped
strawberries or raspberries

1. Place the silicone paper on 2 baking sheets. Set the oven to 100°C/200°F/gas mark 1/2.

2. Whisk the egg whites with a pinch of salt to a stiff snow. Whisk in 30ml/2 tablespoons of the sugar and continue to whisk until the mixture is stiff and shiny. Fold in the remaining sugar with a metal spoon.

3. Put the mixture into a forcing bag fitted with a rose pipe, and pipe on to the silicone paper to form little baskets.

4. Leave to dry in the oven for 2 hours. Take out and allow to cool.

5. Place a little cream in each basket and fill with strawberries or raspberries.

NOTE I: Meringue baskets are often made with meringue cuite (see page 144), which is very solid and does not rise out of shape in the oven.

NOTE II: An electric mixer gives a similar result to meringue cuite, but the hand-made uncooked kind tastes better, even if it looks less professional. If making a meringue mixture in an electric machine, gradually add half the sugar when the whites are stiff, whisk again until very stiff, then whisk in the remaining sugar until just incorporated.

Banana and Grape Vacherin

SERVES 6
4 egg whites
pinch of salt
225g/8oz caster sugar
1 banana
lemon juice
85g/3oz black grapes
85g/3oz green grapes
290ml/ 1/2 pint double cream, lightly whipped

1. Set the oven to 100°C/200°F/gas mark 1/2. Cover 2 baking sheets with silicone paper.

2. Whisk the egg whites with the salt until stiff but not dry, then add 30ml/2 tablespoons of the sugar. Whisk again until very stiff and shiny. Fold in the remaining sugar.

3. Fill a forcing bag fitted with a medium-sized plain nozzle with the meringue. Pipe into 2 rounds the size of a dessert plate.

4. Place in the oven to dry out slowly for 2-3 hours. The meringue is ready when light and dry, and the paper will peel off the underside easily.

5. Cut the banana into chunks and toss in the lemon juice. Halve and deseed the grapes.

6. Spread three-quarters of the cream on one of the meringue cases and scatter over the banana and all but 4 each of the black and green grapes. Place the second meringue on top of this. Using the rest of the cream, pipe rosettes around the top. Decorate each alternate rosette with a grape half.

NOTE: If making a meringue mixture with a powerful electric mixer, gradually add half the sugar when the whites are stiff. Whisk again until very shiny and then add the remaining sugar and whisk lightly until just incorporated.

SWEET WHITE

Hazelnut Meringue Cake with Raspberry Sauce

SERVES 6
110g/4oz hazelnuts
4 egg whites
pinch of salt
225g/8oz caster sugar
drop of vanilla essence
2.5ml/1/2 teaspoon white vinegar
225g/8oz raspberries
icing sugar
squeeze of lemon juice
290ml/1/2 pint double cream

1. Set the oven to 190°C/375°F/gas mark 5. Line 2 x 20cm/8 inch cake tins with lightly oiled tin foil.

2. Place the hazelnuts on a baking sheet and bake until dark brown. Remove the skin by rubbing the nuts in a tea towel. Leave to get completely cold. Set aside 5 nuts and grind the rest. Do not over-grind or they will become greasy and make the meringue heavy. Weigh the nuts. You will need 100g/3½ oz for the meringue.

3. Whisk the egg whites with a pinch of salt until stiff and then gradually beat in the caster sugar a tablespoon at a time, the vanilla and vinegar, beating until very stiff. Fold in the nuts very gently with a large metal spoon. Pile the mixture into the prepared tins, spreading evenly with a spatula.

4. Bake for 40 minutes. Allow to cool in the tin. Lift out the meringues in the tin foil and then peel away all the foil.

5. While the meringue is cooling, liquidize the raspberries with icing sugar and lemon juice. Push through a sieve and taste for sweetness. If very thick, add a little water.

6. To decorate, whip the cream and sandwich the meringue together with two-thirds of it. Dust the top with icing sugar. Pipe 5 large rosettes of cream round the edge of the top of the meringue and decorate each with a reserved hazelnut. Serve the raspberry sauce separately.

RICH SWEET WHITE

Noix au Café

SERVES 4-6
225g/8oz sugar
90-105ml/6-7 tablespoons water
4 egg whites
5ml/1 teaspoon coffee essence

1. Put the sugar and water into a heavy saucepan. Dissolve over a gentle heat and then cook quickly, without stirring, to 116°C/240°F. Use a sugar thermometer for this, or wait until it gets to the soft ball stage (see note on page 142).

2. Whisk the egg whites until stiff. Then pour on the sugar syrup. Pour it steadily on to the egg whites, whisking all the time, but taking care that the syrup does not strike the whisk wires (where it would cool and set solidly). Continue whisking until all the sugar has been absorbed, and the meringue is completely cool. Beat in the coffee essence.

3. Set the oven to 140°C/275°F/gas mark 1. Line 2 baking sheets with bakewell paper (vegetable parchment). Hold in place with a few dots of uncooked meringue.

4. Reserve a quarter of the mixture for the filling. Place the remaining mixture in a forcing bag fitted with a medium-sized plain nozzle. Pipe walnut-sized mounds on the prepared baking sheets.

5. Bake for 1-1$\frac{1}{2}$ hours or until dry and crisp, when they will lift easily off the paper. Then when completely cool, sandwich them together with the reserved coffee meringue mixture.

Pavlova

SERVES 4-6
4 egg whites
pinch of salt
225g/8oz caster sugar
5ml/1 teaspoon cornflour
5ml/1 teaspoon vanilla essence
5ml/1 teaspoon white wine vinegar or
  lemon juice
290ml/$\frac{1}{2}$ pint double cream, lightly whipped
30g/1oz roughly chopped walnuts
450g/1lb fresh pineapple, cored and cut into
  cubes

1. Set the oven to 140°C/275°F/gas mark 1.

2. Put a sheet of silicone paper on a baking sheet.

3. Whisk the egg whites with a pinch of salt until stiff. Gradually add the sugar, beating until you can stand a spoon in the mixture.

4. Add the cornflour, vanilla and vinegar or lemon juice.

5. Pile the mixture on to the prepared baking sheet, shaping to a flat oval or a circle 3cm/1$\frac{1}{2}$ inches thick. Then bake for about 1 hour. The meringue is cooked when the outer shell is pale biscuit coloured and hard to the touch. Remove carefully and gently peel off the paper.

6. When quite cold, spoon on the whipped cream and sprinkle on the fruit and nuts.

NOTE: Any fruits in season can be substituted for nuts and pineapple.

Basic
Recipes

Crème Anglaise (English Egg Custard)

290ml/¹/₂ pint milk
15ml/1 tablespoon sugar
1 vanilla pod or few drops of vanilla essence
2 egg yolks

1. Heat the milk with the sugar and vanilla pod and bring slowly to the boil.
2. Beat the yolks in a bowl. Remove the vanilla pod and pour the milk on to the egg yolks, stirring steadily. Mix well and return to the pan.
3. Stir over gentle heat until the mixture thickens so that it will coat the back of a spoon; this will take about 5 minutes. Do not boil.
4. Pour into a cold bowl.
5. Add the vanilla essence if using.

Crème Pâtissière

290ml/¹/₂ pint milk
2 egg yolks
55g/2oz caster sugar
20g/³/₄oz flour
20g/³/₄oz cornflour
vanilla essence

1. Scald the milk. Then cream the egg yolks with the sugar and when pale, mix in the flours.
2. Pour on the milk and mix well.
3. Return the mixture to the pan and bring slowly up to the boil, stirring continuously. (It will go alarmingly lumpy, but don't worry, keep stirring and it will get smooth.)
4. Allow to cool slightly and add the vanilla essence.

Crème Chantilly

150ml/¹/₄ pint double cream
30ml/2 tablespoons iced water
5ml/1 teaspoon icing sugar
2 drops vanilla essence

1. Put all the ingredients into a chilled bowl and whisk with a balloon whisk, steadily but not too fast, for about 2 minutes or until the cream has thickened and doubled in volume.
2. Whisk faster for 30-40 seconds until the mixture is very fluffy and will form soft peaks.
NOTE: Chilling the ingredients and the bowl gives a lighter, whiter result.

Glacé Icing

225g/8oz icing sugar
boiling water

1. Sift the icing sugar into a bowl.
2. Add enough boiling water to mix to a fairly stiff coating consistency. The icing should hold a trail when dropped from a spoon but gradually find its own level. It needs surprisingly little water.
NOTE: Hot water produces a shinier result than cold. Also, the icing, on drying, is less likely to craze, crack or become watery if made with boiling water.

Soured Cream and Chocolate Icing

140g/5oz plain chocolate
150ml/¹/₄ pint soured cream
10ml/2 teaspoons caster sugar

1. Break up the chocolate and place in a double saucepan. Add the soured cream and sugar. Melt together over a gentle heat. Leave to cool and thicken.

Sugar Syrup

285g/10oz granulated sugar
570ml/1 pint water
pared rind of 1 lemon

1. Put the sugar, water and lemon rind in a pan and heat slowly until the sugar has completely dissolved.
2. Bring to the boil and cook to the required consistency. Allow to cool, then strain. Keep covered in a cool place until needed.
NOTE: Sugar syrup will keep unrefrigerated for about 5 days, and for several weeks if kept cold.

Raspberry Coulis

340g/12oz fresh raspberries
juice of 1/2 lemon
70ml/2 1/2 fl oz sugar syrup (see above)

1. Whizz all the ingredients together in a food processor, and push through a conical strainer.
NOTE: If it is too thin, it can be thickened by boiling rapidly in a heavy saucepan. Stir well to prevent it 'catching'.

Redcurrant glaze

60ml/4 tablespoons redcurrant jelly
15ml/1 tablespoon lemon juice

1. To make the glaze: melt the redcurrant

jelly with the lemon juice, but do not allow it to boil. Keep warm.

Lemon Curd

MAKES 450g/1lb
2 large lemons
85g/3oz butter
225g/8oz granulated sugar
3 eggs

1. Grate the rind of the lemons on the finest gauge on the grater, taking care to grate the rind only, not the pith.
2. Squeeze the juice from the lemons.
3. Put the rind, juice, butter, sugar and lightly beaten eggs into a heavy saucepan or double boiler and heat gently, stirring all the time until the mixture is thick.
4. Strain into jam jars and cover.
NOTE I: This curd will keep in the refrigerator for about 3 weeks.
NOTE II: If the curd is boiled, no great harm is done, as the acid and sugar prevent the eggs from scrambling.

Apricot Glaze

45ml/3 tablespoons apricot jam
30ml/2 tablespoons water
juice of 1/2 lemon

1. Place all the ingredients together in a thick-bottomed pan.
2. Bring slowly up to the boil, stirring gently (avoid beating in bubbles) until syrupy in consistency. Strain.
NOTE: When using this to glaze food, use when still warm, as it becomes too stiff to manage when cold. It will keep warm standing over a saucepan of very hot water.

Apple Marmalade

3 cooking apples
a little butter
strip of lemon rind
about 85g/3oz brown sugar

1. Wash the unpeeled apples, quarter and core them. Rub the bottom and sides of a heavy saucepan with butter.
2. Slice the apples thickly into the pan and add the lemon rind.
3. Cover and cook gently, stirring occasionally, until completely soft.
4. Push through a sieve. Rinse out the pan and return the purée to it. Add at least 55g/2oz brown sugar to 570ml/1 pint purée. Cook rapidly until the mixture is of dropping consistency (about 4 minutes). Allow to cool. Add more sugar if necessary.

Marzipan or Almond Paste (Uncooked)

225g/8oz caster sugar
225g/8oz icing sugar
450g/1lb ground almonds
2 egg yolks
2 whole eggs
10ml/2 teaspoons lemon juice
6 drops vanilla essence

1. Sift the sugars together into a bowl and mix with the ground almonds.
2. Mix together the egg yolks, whole eggs, lemon juice and vanilla essence. Add this to the sugar mixture and beat briefly with a wooden spoon.
3. Lightly dust the working surface with icing sugar.
4. Knead the paste until just smooth

(overworking will draw the oil out of the almonds, giving a too greasy paste).
5. Wrap well and store in a cool place.

Whisked Sponge

3 eggs
85g/3oz caster sugar
22.5ml/1¹/₂ tablespoons lukewarm water
85g/3oz plain flour, sifted
pinch of salt

1. Set the oven to 180°C/350°F/gas mark 4. Prepare a cake tin (see page 40).
2. Place the eggs and sugar in a bowl and fit it over (not in) a saucepan of simmering water. Whisk the mixture until light, thick and fluffy. (If using an electric mixer no heat is required.)
3. Remove the bowl from the heat and continue whisking until slightly cooled. Add the water.
4. Sift the flour and salt and, with a large metal spoon, fold into the mixture, being careful not to beat out any of the air.
5. Turn the mixture into the prepared tin and bake in the middle of the oven for about 30 minutes.
6. Test to see if it is cooked. (When the cake is ready, it will shrink slightly and the edges will look crinkled. When pressed gently it will feel firm but spongy and will sound 'creaky'.)
7. Turn out on to a wire rack to cool.

Aubergine and Chestnut Pie

For the aubergine layer:
1 medium-sized aubergine, cut into cubes
85ml/3fl oz olive oil

3 tomatoes, roughly chopped
30ml/2 tablespoons tomato purée
1 garlic clove, crushed
15ml/1 tablespoon fresh basil, chopped
15ml/1 tablespoon fresh marjoram,
  chopped
salt and freshly ground black pepper

For the nut layer:
1 small onion, finely chopped
2 sticks celery, finely chopped
55ml/4 fl oz water
110g/4oz walnuts, roughly chopped
110g/4oz unsweetened chestnut purée
55g/2oz peeled and cooked chestnuts,
  roughly chopped (see note)
30g/1oz fresh wholemeal bread cubes

For the courgette layer:
225g/8oz courgettes, sliced
1 small bunch chives, finely chopped
15ml/1 tablespoon single cream
salt and freshly ground black pepper

To finish:
45ml/3 tablespoons oil
7 sheets filo pastry
15g/1 tablespoon sesame seeds

1. Put the aubergines into a colander.
Sprinkle with salt and leave to stand for 20
minutes. Then preheat the oven to
200°C/400°F/gas mark 6.
2. Rinse the aubergines and pat dry. Fry
them in three-quarters of the oil until
beginning to soften, add the tomatoes,
tomato purée, garlic, basil and marjoram.
Season with salt and pepper and cook
gently until tender.
3. Make the nut layer. Cook the onions and
celery in the oil until soft. Add the water,
walnuts, chestnut purée, chestnuts, bread
cubes, salt and pepper. Cook for 2-3
minutes.
4. Sauté the courgettes in the remaining oil.

When tender add the cream, chives, salt
and pepper.
5. Layer the fillings up in a large dish,
starting with the aubergines and finishing
with the courgettes. Then cover the pie
with 7 layers of filo pastry, brushing each
layer with oil. Brush the top with oil and
sprinkle with the sesame seeds. Then bake
for 20 minutes or until the top is
golden brown.
NOTE: To get 55g/2 oz of peeled cooked
chestnuts you will need to buy about
170g/6oz of fresh chestnuts. To cook
them, make a slit in the skin of each
chestnut, and put them into a pan of cold
water. Bring to the boil, simmer for 10
minutes, and then take off the heat.
Remove 1 or 2 nuts at a time and peel – the
skins come off quite easily if the chestnuts
are hot but not overcooked.

Cheese Soufflé

SERVES 2
40g/1 1/4oz butter
dry white breadcrumbs
30g/1oz flour
2.5ml/1/2 teaspoon made English mustard
pinch of cayenne pepper
290ml/1/2 pint milk
85g/3oz strong Cheddar or Gruyère cheese,
  grated
4 eggs, separated
salt and pepper

1. Set the oven to 200°C/400°F/gas mark 6.
Melt a knob of the butter and brush out a
15cm/6 inch soufflé dish with it. Dust
lightly with the breadcrumbs.
2. Melt the rest of the butter in a saucepan
and stir in the flour, mustard and cayenne
pepper. Cook for 45 seconds. Add the milk
and cook, stirring vigorously, for 2

minutes. The mixture will get very thick and leave the sides of the pan. Take it off the heat.

3. Stir in the cheese, egg yolks, salt and pepper. Taste; the mixture should be very well seasoned.

4. Whisk the egg whites until stiff, but not dry, and mix a spoonful into the mixture. Then fold in the rest and pour into the soufflé dish, which should be about two-thirds full. Run your finger around the top of the soufflé mixture. This gives a 'top hat' appearance to the cooked soufflé.

5. Bake for 25-30 minutes and serve straight away. (Do not test to see if the soufflé is done for a least 20 minutes. Then open the oven just wide enough to get your hand in and give the soufflé a slight shove. If it wobbles alarmingly, cook a further 5 minutes.)

Index